D0566230

AMERICA'S

Inland
Waterway

EXPLORING THE ATLANTIC SEABOARD

By ALLAN C. FISHER, JR.
Photographed by JAMES L. AMOS
Foreword by CORNELIUS SHIELDS

Prepared by the Special Publications Division
National Geographic Society, Washington, D. C.

AMERICA'S INLAND WATERWAY:
Exploring the Atlantic Seaboard

By ALLAN C. FISHER, JR.
National Geographic Senior Assistant Editor
Photographed by JAMES L. AMOS
National Geographic Photographer

Published by
THE NATIONAL GEOGRAPHIC SOCIETY
MELVIN M. PAYNE, *President*
MELVILLE BELL GROSVENOR, *Editor-in-Chief*
GILBERT M. GROSVENOR, *Editor*
JOHN SCOFIELD, *Consulting Editor*

Prepared by
THE SPECIAL PUBLICATIONS DIVISION
ROBERT L. BREEDEN, *Editor*
DONALD J. CRUMP, *Associate Editor*
PHILIP B. SILCOTT, *Senior Editor*
MERRILL WINDSOR, *Managing Editor*
LINDA M. BRIDGE, *Assistant to the Editor
    and Chief Researcher*
WENDY W. CORTESI, MARGERY G. DUNN,
    LOUISA V. MAGZANIAN, JENNIFER
    URQUHART, *Researchers*
VIRGINIA H. FINNEGAN, *Assistant to the Author*

Illustrations
WILLIAM L. ALLEN, *Picture Editor*
LINDA M. BRIDGE, WENDY W. CORTESI, MARGERY
    G. DUNN, JOAN REINACH, JUDITH E. RINARD,
    MICHAEL W. ROBBINS, *Picture Legends*

Design and Art Direction
CHARLES O. HYMAN, *Designer*
CONNIE BROWN, *Assistant Designer*
JOHN D. GARST, JR., VIRGINIA L. BAZA,
    MARGARET A. DEANE, NANCY SCHWEICKART,
    SNEJINKA STEFANOFF, MILDA R. STONE,
    Map Research, Design, and Production

Production and Printing
ROBERT W. MESSER, *Production Manager*
GEORGE V. WHITE, *Assistant Production Manager*
MARGARET MURIN SKEKEL, MARY L. BERNARD,
    RAJA D. MURSHED, *Production Assistants*
JOHN R. METCALFE, *Engraving and Printing*
JANE H. BUXTON, MARTA ISABEL COONS,
    CAROL A. ENQUIST, SUZANNE J. JACOBSON,
    PENELOPE A. LOEFFLER, JOAN PERRY,
    MARILYN L. WILBUR, *Staff Assistants*
TONI WARNER, ANNE MCCAIN, *Index*

Copyright © 1973 National Geographic Society. All rights
reserved. Reproduction of the whole or any part of the
contents without written permission is prohibited.
Library of Congress CIP Data: page 207

HARD-COVER DESIGN: ISKANDAR BADAY

*Approaching home port near Annapolis,
Maryland, author-skipper Allan Fisher and
first mate Bill Gay head* Andromeda *toward the
entrance to the South River from Chesapeake
Bay. Accompanied by Fisher's wife, Mike,
they spent six months aboard the 43-foot
motorsailer cruising the Atlantic Intracoastal
Waterway between Massachusetts and Florida.
Overleaf: At twilight a flight of geese soars high
above the Eastern Shore of the Chesapeake,
where quiet waters provide safe anchorage.
Page 1: Cormorants perch on a "dolphin"
supporting an Intracoastal Waterway navigational aid that warns boatmen away from
a shoal off Key Largo in Florida Bay.*

Foreword

*M*any yachtsmen, I fear, would consider a trip between New England and Florida by way of the Atlantic Intracoastal Waterway a drab and tiresome prospect—until they open this book. Whoever has fostered that false impression must never have taken time to explore the inviting passages and secluded communities that exist in abundance along the route. Allan Fisher's story and the photographs by Jim Amos show clearly that the Inland Waterway, far from being a dull route to be endured to reach a destination, is a fascinating cruising ground in its own right.

Allan has made me envious and perhaps a little wistful with his appealing descriptions of the lovely waters and anchorages he has found. My own experience with the regions he describes is confined primarily to the areas within New England and Long Island Sound; those are dearest to my heart from lifelong association. I have cruised and raced in them all dozens and dozens of times. In my rather limited traveling in this country and abroad, I have never seen other waters or coasts that equal them. Perhaps I am biased because they have given me so much real joy, but I truly believe that for any sailor, especially in the company of his family, these waters offer as much of the excitement and serenity of cruising as any others I know.

Now, after reading this book, I realize that such opportunities lie along the entire East Coast of our country.

Long Island Sound is my special love. The Larchmont Yacht Club is my home port. I will be everlastingly grateful for the pleasure that both have afforded me over the years. The thing that I like best about the Sound is that it is never the same—especially when I am sailing. Just a shift of wind or tide, or a different tack, keeps the Sound a new, ever-changing experience. The winter races we call "frostbiting" are among my fondest memories. They provide excellent training and marvelous fun, and make possible year-round sailing. There are endless adventures to be enjoyed while cruising the Sound's shorelines and poking into hidden harbors and cozy inlets. Allan's account of these places I know so well has enhanced my own appreciation of them.

Too often many of us sail our waters like motorists on a superhighway: Conscious only of our destination, we pass by the many joys of nature that lie just off the road. In this book, Allan Fisher and Jim Amos give us a view of the Inland Waterway that reveals the beauty and contentment available to anyone who will take the time to seek them.

CORNELIUS SHIELDS

Brown pelicans, an endangered species, roost undisturbed in Pelican Island National Wildlife Refuge on the

Contents

Indian River in Florida.

Skimming over Biscayne Bay, a jaunty catamaran skirts the Waterway near Miami, Florida.

$\mathcal{P}rologue$

$\mathcal{T}$he Atlantic Intracoastal Waterway is not one route but many; it presents not a single challenge but a succession; it shows not just a few faces or moods but a multitude. For the Waterway can be open water and distant headland, a place of maddened seas and stinging spray and unrelenting wind—yet it is also the fragile mirror of a canal or a creek devoid of wind, with water so sheltered that the wake of a boat seems a violent intrusion. It is the skyline of New York City and the soaring canopies of great bridges—and the maze of a shadowed swamp where gaunt cypresses thrust centipede legs into water the color of strong tea. It is a glorified ditch walled in by hives of masonry called condominiums—and a broad sound or a lovely river where the traveler journeys mile after mile past wooded shores that bear no trace of man's despoiling presence.

The Waterway is a sail through history as well as geography, through the hard and painful birth of our nation and through warfare that shaped our destiny. It is the workaday present, a series of changing cities and busy towns. It is clean water and polluted water, crowded marinas and quiet, solitary anchorages, noisome factories and shoreside farms, fishermen and water skiers, tugboats and barges and plush yachts, and surely some of the most bizarre characters who have ever trod a deck or set a sail.

Maps usually show the Waterway as a red line running down the East Coast of the United States, remaining inside the boundary of land and sea wherever possible and in no instance venturing far offshore. It begins at the Annisquam River, 26 miles northeast of Boston, and winds its sinuous way 2,000 miles to Key West—though much of the passage through Florida Bay is shallow and snaggly with coral.

In its northern reaches the route passes through many miles of open and relatively unprotected waters: Massachusetts Bay, Buzzards Bay, Block Island Sound, Long Island Sound, the Atlantic Ocean off New Jersey (if one has too much boat to travel the Garden State's shallow inside passage), Delaware Bay, and that big inland sea, the Chesapeake. From Norfolk to Miami it takes advantage of innumerable rivers, creeks, sounds, inlets, bays, and estuaries, stitched together wherever necessary by man-made cuts.

Artery of commerce, small-boat thoroughfare and haven, water playground, safe passage to the sun: Call it what you will, it adds up to a magnificent facility. The U. S. Army Corps of Engineers and the U. S. Coast Guard share responsibility for the Waterway, as they do for all our navigable inland waters. The Corps plans, constructs, maintains, operates, and improves it; the Coast Guard tends the navigational markers, and gets boatmen out of trouble when they get into it, which is often.

Centuries ago Indians used the coastal and inland waters of the Atlantic seaboard for communication. So did Europeans once they gained a foothold on the continent's edge. They soon saw the advantage of connecting various natural waterways. In 1643 colonists dug a narrow canal the half mile between the Annisquam River and Gloucester Harbor in Massachusetts; small craft then could avoid the long trip around Cape Ann. Today that segment is believed to be the oldest man-made portion of the Intracoastal Waterway.

Atlantic Intracoastal Waterway

0-60
60-120
120-300
300-2,000

DEPTHS IN FEET

Sometime before 1800, planters in South Carolina dug three small canals at points where rivers came close enough together to invite connection; these too are now part of the route. A canal across Cape Cod was proposed as early as 1676, though it did not become a reality until early in this century. Work began in 1793 on the Dismal Swamp Canal in Virginia and North Carolina. Built by slave labor, it opened in 1805 to shallow-draft boats. In 1829 a toll-lock canal connecting the Delaware River and Chesapeake Bay began operation.

These were all private ventures. Not until 1828 and the enlarging of the water route between Cumberland Sound in Georgia and Florida's St. Johns River did the Federal Government engage in any actual work on what is now the Atlantic Intracoastal Waterway—also known as the Inland Waterway. But by then a grand design had begun to emerge, and slowly, step by difficult and costly step, it became a reality.

By 1940 the route was essentially complete. Today, except for the shallow passage in New Jersey, the Waterway provides a minimum depth of 12 feet as far south as Fort Pierce, Florida, and a minimum channel width of 90 feet as far as Miami. The Corps of Engineers has asked for funds to deepen the Fort Pierce-to-Miami section to 12 feet.

My home waters are those of Chesapeake Bay; I live on Church

Creek, a beautiful little tidal stream off Maryland's South River, a Chesapeake tributary. The 200-mile-long Bay is a part of the Waterway that I know intimately. I had never done any extensive boating elsewhere on the Intracoastal, however, until two years ago.

I had long wanted to. In autumn, when ducks and geese winged in dark skeins across Chesapeake skies, I watched yachting's gold-platers and cockleshells cruise by me, heading south. In early spring, when the shadbush put forth delicate little white blossoms along Chesapeake shores, I saw the first of the water gypsies moving north. In 1972 the Norfolk District of the Corps of Engineers counted nearly 10,000 pleasure boats passing through, north and south, on the Waterway. Ah, to be part of that armada!

Well, why not? Why not take six months and gather material for a book? Start in New England and cruise leisurely south to Miami, stopping wherever and whenever I might wish. And why not take my wife, Mike, along? Actually I hardly ever sail without her. Mike (the nickname derives from her maiden name, Michael) has had a love affair with wide waters, particularly the Chesapeake, from childhood. She readily joined my crew for the Waterway trip as chief cook and counselor.

But we also needed a male hand, preferably young, agile, and without paunch. So we signed aboard William Childs Gay, 21-year-old son of our next-door neighbors on Church Creek. Bill took a semester off from his senior year at Hampden-Sydney College to serve as first mate. The three of us made the entire trip, though we often had others aboard, notably National Geographic photographer Jim Amos, a seasoned skipper himself.

We sailed in a spanking new boat, a 43-foot Gulfstar motorsailer, the second boat I have owned named *Andromeda*. Sloop-rigged, with a center cockpit, fore and aft cabins, and dependable 120-horsepower diesel, she proved a good sailer and a comfortable home afloat.

A water route so long and varied is not without hazard. Despite the common appelation Inland Waterway, the suggestion of protected waters is more appropriate to the southern reaches than to the northern; and even the portion south of Norfolk has its troublesome and boisterous spots. Shallow Albemarle Sound in North Carolina is considered by many—including me—to be

Sails filled by a strong breeze, Allan Fisher's sloop-rigged motorsailer Andromeda *scuds across Chesapeake Bay. Opposite: The Atlantic Intracoastal Waterway extends 2,000 miles from Massachusetts to the Florida Keys.*

Luxurious havens like Pier 66 (above) in Fort Lauderdale, Florida, welcome visitors with an array of amenities. In addition to boat slips and complete repair facilities, many marinas provide electric outlets, extension telephones, water connections, ice, grocery deliveries, swimming pools, restaurants, and hotel accommodations. At Bahia Mar, Fort Lauderdale's largest marina (opposite, above), amateur barber Janet Snyder promptly sets up shop wherever she finds a customer in need of a haircut. Demand for experienced crewmen peaks before a long-distance yacht race such as the biennial run from Newport, Rhode Island, to Bermuda. The day before the start, hopeful sailors (opposite) roam the Newport docks advertising their abilities and looking for positions to fill.

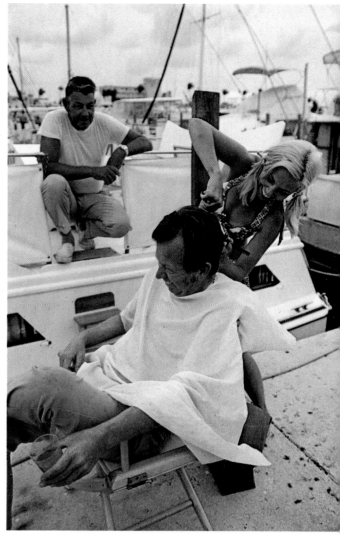

the most treacherous body of water on the East Coast. Still, a skipper with a modest amount of experience and a sound, dependably powered boat can cruise safely anywhere on the Waterway, north or south, if he scrupulously checks weather forecasts before venturing long runs in open water. He may get caught offshore a time or two in squalls, but fortunately such storms usually are brief.

I hope many who read this book will want to follow in *Andromeda*'s wake. But first, one caution: This is not a guide directing you to marinas and anchorages and describing channels and routes and hazards. This is a travel book, the story of one boat and its cruise. We did not go everywhere we could have gone or perhaps should have gone. You may prefer to call at places we bypassed.

Any boatman will find such a cruise one of the most rewarding he has ever made.

"Messing about" in a small boat is fun in itself, of course, but that's not the whole explanation of boating's appeal. I firmly believe communication among water-going people is warmer, franker, easier, and friendlier than it is among folks ashore. The cheery wave, the smiling greeting, the quick help to those in trouble, the swapping of good yarns—these things are still traditional among boatmen even if increasingly hard to find elsewhere in our society.

I am convinced, too, that boating is popular because it satisfies some deep need in many of us. What I mean can be illustrated by the story of a friend of mine who worked for a big and impersonal public utility company. His job was demanding and he worked under extreme pressure; and as he grew older, he came to dislike intensely his trouble-shooting, problem-solving role and his abrasive boss.

My friend had never sailed, but one day, while in an anguish of spirit for which there seemed no solace, he agreed to go on a weekend cruise. Perhaps the fresh air would help. Leaving the harbor, he saw a sign on the shore that displayed the name of his company, and for a moment he felt a tightening vise in the pit of his stomach.

Forty-eight hours later, returning to port, he saw the same sign, but this time he could say to his friends with wonder, "Why, I didn't think of a single miserable office problem for two whole days!"

So he bought a boat, and nine years later he is still one of the most avid sailors on the Chesapeake. He had learned that wonderful thing about boating: Somehow it has the power not only to refresh but also to heal. Your troubles remain ashore, and you become intent on small things: the set of a sail, the flight of a bird, a shift of the wind, the next buoy. Sky, water, wave-lashed rock, that lovely shore . . . for a time they are all yours, and they set you free.

Fresh spring foliage gree.

llan Fisher and Bill Gay as they secure **Andromeda** *at her home dock on Church Creek, Maryland.*

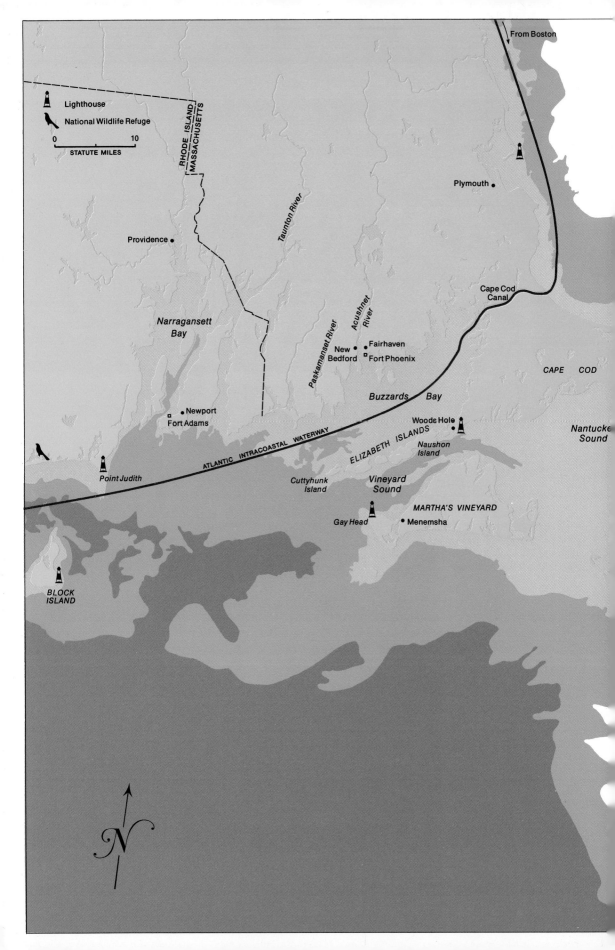

From Boston

Lighthouse
National Wildlife Refuge

0   10
STATUTE MILES

RHODE ISLAND
MASSACHUSETTS

Taunton River

Plymouth ●

Providence ●

Narragansett
Bay

Cape Cod
Canal

Paskamanset River
Acushnet River

New
Bedford ● ● Fairhaven
□ Fort Phoenix

CAPE   COD

Buzzards   Bay

Newport ●
□
Fort Adams

Woods Hole
● ▲

Nantucket
Sound

ATLANTIC   INTRACOASTAL   WATERWAY

ELIZABETH   ISLANDS

Naushon
Island

Point Judith

Cuttyhunk
Island

Vineyard
Sound

MARTHA'S VINEYARD

Gay Head

● Menemsha

BLOCK
ISLAND

N

1

New England:
In the Wake
of the Whalers

*Atlantic Intracoastal
Waterway provides varied
cruising and vigorous sport
in the open waters off
Massachusetts and Rhode
Island. Short side trips lead
to historic ports of call.*

*A*ll day a heavy fog had possessed the sea, making it indistinguishable from the sodden gray of air and sky. But now, in midafternoon, the fog thinned and lifted. Suddenly the sun broke through, and there she came: a big, three-masted sailing ship, her hull growing steadily larger as the sun scoured a path for her over the sea.

For two hours I had been among a crowd of hundreds keeping vigil from the ruins of old Fort Phoenix at the entrance to the inner harbor of New Bedford, Massachusetts. Below us a flotilla of stubby fishing boats slipped through the gate in the harbor's hurricane barrier and scurried out to escort the bark. All flew the Portuguese flag, and bright signal pennants streamed from their rigging. The leader, a husky trawler named *Portugal*, bore atop her wheelhouse a large design of paper flowers displaying the cross of the Portuguese Order of Christ. She and her companions deployed themselves off the larger vessel's high stern like fat little ducks in the wake of a swan.

The splendid *Sagres*, a training vessel of the Portuguese Navy, is one of the last of the tall ships. How I wished I could see her great sails billow to a stiff following wind! But the breeze was bow on, only the softest exhalation of the north wind, and her sails lay lifeless and tightly furled along her yards. Slowly, hardly leaving a wake, she approached the barrier under power.

Even bereft of wind, she looked lovely and impressive, her 293-foot hull gleaming white and unmarred, her huge bowsprit flaring sharply up like a cannon trained on heaven, her ratlines, shrouds, stays, and halyards forming a complex web. A bosun's whistle sounded shrilly, and her cadets and sailors, all in dress whites, mustered on the deck in disciplined ranks.

Sagres pushed her bow through the gate. At that moment, her escorts and scores of fishing boats and yachts lying in the harbor let loose with bells and whistles, *(Continued on page 23)*

Wooded shoreline of beech and oak rims Tarpaulin Cove, a secluded anchorage on Naushon Island across fro

Martha's Vineyard. Summer residents share the island, largest of the Elizabeth chain, with sheep and wildlife.

SCRIMSHAW EXAMPLES: NEW BEDFORD WHALING MUSEUM

Vivid reminders of the Yankee whaler's quest for blubber and bone are carefully preserved in New Bedford's Whaling Museum, Free Public Library, and private collections. Miss Sylvia Knowles (above) studies a ship's log for 1874-79, handed down through several generations of her family. An illustrated log page (below) from the New Bedford bark **Lafayette** records an unsuccessful attempt to kill a sperm whale off the coast of Peru in 1842. Whaling voyages, often lasting three or four years, inevitably brought long periods of idleness between sightings. To relieve the tedium, sailors using jackknives and other simple tools developed the distinctive art form of scrimshaw, the carving of whale teeth and bone. Sperm-whale ivory provided material for the minutely detailed scene above and the bird-in-flight "jagging wheel," or pie crimper, carved about 1850.

Opposite, young visitors in the New Bedford Whaling Museum gaze up into the rigging of a half-scale model of the **Lagoda**, veteran of 12 voyages and one of the most successful whaling ships to sail from New Bedford.

MELVILLE WHALING ROOM, NEW BEDFORD FREE PUBLIC LIBRARY

and she replied with the deep growl of her horn. Now that the barrier was passing abeam, *Sagres* had officially arrived. An old friend had returned to New Bedford.

One of several former whaling ports along the Atlantic Intracoastal Waterway, New Bedford has 16,000 Portuguese-Americans in its population of 102,000. Many are fishermen, and they man most of the harbor's fleet of some 130 fishing vessels. When *Sagres* is in port, as she has been several times while on goodwill cruises to the United States, not many fish get caught; the town is busy entertaining her officers, crew, and cadets.

*B*ut I suspect the welcome would be just as warm without the tie to Portugal. Few ports in America have a seafaring tradition as remarkable as that of New Bedford. For years the city reigned as the world's foremost whaling port. In 1857 some 330 whaleships operated from here, more than from all other American ports combined, and 10,000 seamen served aboard the city's whalers. But in 1859, petroleum was discovered in Pennsylvania, and whaling's long decline began.

At its height New Bedford was one of the most colorful maritime crossroads on earth. Herman Melville, describing its polyglot waterfront in his whaling classic, *Moby Dick*, wrote:

"In thoroughfares nigh the docks, any considerable seaport will frequently offer to view the queerest looking nondescripts from foreign parts. . . . but in New Bedford, actual cannibals stand chatting at street corners; savages outright; many of whom yet carry on their bones unholy flesh. It makes a stranger stare."

That era of the great sea hunt is now but a memory. It came to an end on August 20, 1925, with the return of the schooner *John R. Manta* from the last whaling voyage out of New Bedford. But the town's kinship with the sea, its mystical feeling for ships and sailors, endures. When a wonderful windjammer like *Sagres* enters that harbor, her crew know they belong.

A cadet from *Sagres*, whom I stopped briefly on the waterfront, expressed that kinship well. A fisherman interpreted for us, for the lad spoke little English, though with his blond, short-cut hair he looked like a midshipman from the United States Naval Academy at Annapolis, near my home.

"Our ship bears the name of a place very important in Portuguese history," he said. "In Sagres lived Prince Henry the Navigator. There he ran a school of navigation and sent out ships and captains to explore. Your New Bedford is like our Sagres — a place of maritime history, of proud beginnings."

From New Bedford, Melville sailed aboard *Acushnet*, the whaling vessel that provided much of the material for *Moby Dick*. For a time he lived in Fairhaven, just across the Acushnet River from New Bedford. In a field in Fairhaven, a ship captain named Joshua Slocum rebuilt the old sloop *Spray* before setting out in that 37-foot boat on the first solo circumnavigation of the world, a voyage of more than three years that began in

Storm barrier with swinging gates extends across the Acushnet River, providing flood protection from high tides for low-lying areas of New Bedford and Fairhaven. The mill-town complex in the foreground dates from the late 1800's, when textile manufacturing had replaced whaling as New Bedford's major industry. Demand for whale oil fell steadily after the 1859 discovery of petroleum in Pennsylvania.

In calm seas off Martha's Vineyard, lobsterman Donald Poole hauls in his string of pots, or traps, before moving them to a new location. Colorful buoys attached to the traps identify the owner. Massachusetts law allows him to keep and sell both male and female lobsters over a specified size — except for egg-bearing females, which he promptly returns to the water. At left, tails of swordfish caught by F. Stuart Knight decorate his boathouse in the Vineyard fishing village of Menemsha.

1895 and resulted in one of the most appealing of adventure books: *Sailing Alone Around the World.*

Slocum's love for the boat he had restored with his own hands became legendary. He wrote an appendix to his book describing *Spray's* design and sail plan so that others could copy her, and he made her his home.

Similarly, my crew and I developed affection and respect for the boat that was our home for six months and carried us safely 3,800 nautical miles. In St. Petersburg, Florida, we had watched her being built, from the moment the 43- by 14-foot fiberglass hull emerged from its mold to the commissioning trials.

Technically *Andromeda* is a motorsailer. Many boats of that breed sail well enough on a reach—that is, when the wind is abeam—and they may run before a following breeze with coltish abandon; yet, on a course to windward, nearly all motorsailers sail badly, and some won't do it at all. *Andromeda*, however, puts her nose on the wind and moves well. With that desirable quality in mind, we had her rigged as a sloop and not a ketch, since a sloop rig will sail "higher": closer to the direction from which the wind blows.

On her foredeck she carries a big, roller-furled genoa. Below the cockpit is the "iron sail," her diesel engine.

In her two cabins *Andromeda* has bunks for six, two heads, two showers, a big dinette area, and a chart table. In good weather the spacious cockpit serves as reception area, living room, and dining room. When we were at dockside or at anchor, Mike would vanish below and soon a hot gourmet meal would be passed topside on trays. She became extremely efficient in her compact, well-equipped galley.

*W*hen I set out to explore New Bedford harbor, I had a knowledgeable guide, civil engineer Fred Tibbetts, who gave me a tour in his powerboat *Teco IV.* We found the city's commercial trawlers rafted up alongside one another at dock after dock, as lifeless as ghost ships, for a strike of fish handlers had idled the fleet. We passed rotting piers, old hulks, and abandoned shoreside buildings—since cleared away for urban renewal—and cruised by long, tin-roofed fish-processing factories.

As we circled the harbor, I thought ahead to the long voyage south, the adventure just beginning. What a fitting place to launch it!—not just because of New Bedford's seafaring traditions, or Melville, or Slocum, but also because here began one of the earliest voyages by a pleasure boat down the Waterway. In an eight-month period in 1912-13, Henry M. Plummer sailed from New Bedford to Miami and back again in a beamy, 24-foot catboat called *Mascot.* Aboard were his 15-year-old son, Henry Jr., and a cat named Scotty. From the log of that voyage came a slender volume, *The Boy, Me and the Cat*, a story of idyllic cruising and near disaster, of humor and pathos, of temporary defeats and ultimate triumph.

Plummer and his son left a New Bedford boatyard and sailed to his farm home on the Paskamanset River to take aboard supplies and the cat. On October 14 he entered in his log:

"Mighty busy cup o' tea this morning. Tumbled all the 'last things' on board. Crawled under the shed, caught the cat, rubbed her full of flea powder, and dropped her into a gunny sack to moult. Will have troubles enough without fleas.

"Good-bye to brave mother, and with a white apron waving from the cottage door, we slipped moorings and stood to sea with fair tide and light westerly breezes."

Often on our own journey we would get out the log of the *Mascot* and read of her adventures in the waters we cruised. Now, at her starting point, I saluted the skill and determination of the Plummers, who sailed a Waterway mostly undredged, unmarked, and untamed.

Fred Tibbets took *Teco IV* down the Acushnet for a closer look at *Sagres*. Near her the *Shenandoah*, a 108-foot cruise vessel, had briefly dropped anchor. *Shenandoah* carries a square-rigged topsail and topgallant; so here, side by side, lay two square-riggers, a rare sight in any waters today. Then *Shenandoah's* yawl boat pushed her past the storm barrier, her crew dressed her with canvas, and she slipped away on the first breath of the night wind.

Today much of New Bedford's waterfront has the look of neglect, but that is changing. The old sector is eligible for designation as a national historic district, thanks to restoration efforts of WHALE, the Waterfront Historic Area League.

Up on Johnny Cake Hill stands the Whaling Museum of the Old Dartmouth Historical Society. I walked in the front entrance, halted abruptly, and stared: Before me a fully rigged bark, with many of her sails set, seemed to be coursing right through the hall, and a score of people strode her decks.

When the gatekeeper finally got my attention and admission fee, he laughed and said, "Nearly all first visitors react that way. She's yar, that one, a great old girl."

A vessel that is "yar" is just about everything she ought to be, and I could understand why the man would say that, even though water had never touched the stout black and white hull. She was, of course, a model, the largest ship model in the world.

Chief medicine man of the Gay Head Indians, Napoleon Bonaparte Madison linked modern Martha's Vineyard with the age of whalers until his death in 1973. In 1905 he sailed from New Bedford as a harpooner on a voyage that lasted two years.

Overleaf: Gay Head cliffs rise abruptly above the waters of Vineyard Sound. Geologists believe that glaciers pressed the clay layers into wavelike folds.

There, in one-half scale, 89 feet from flying jib-boom to spanker boom's end, sailed *Lagoda*, one of the most successful ships that ever flensed a whale. She netted her owners a huge profit on all but one of 12 voyages between 1841 and 1886.

On *Lagoda*'s deck I recognized a pleasant, pervasive odor: hemp and tar. Thanks to her authentic ratlines, shrouds, and other rigging, she even smelled like an old sailing vessel.

Next to me a small boy looked speculatively at the ladder-like ratlines running up the forward mast from a bulkhead, and I noticed that his mother quickly grasped him by the hand. Later I asked Richard C. Kugler, the museum director, if he ever had to chase people out of *Lagoda*'s rigging.

"We once had an entire ship's company of Thai sailors here," he answered. "Suddenly they were all over that rigging. Everywhere you looked a sailor scrambled or swung. But as it turned out, they did no harm. That rigging is strong; she was rigged in the old way by experts."

Across a cobblestone street from the museum stands the Seamen's Bethel, an austere, gray clapboard chapel built in 1832 and immortalized by Melville in *Moby Dick*. Its pulpit, as described by Melville, looked like a ship's bow with bowsprit. That pulpit was a product of the author's imagination, but in the chapel I stood in front of one very like it, built many years after publication of the book so that fact would correspond to the more compelling reality of the fictional classic.

I thought the pulpit-bow an inspired creation by the author; from time beyond history, sailors have sought the bow of a ship to ask: What am I? Where am I going? I have often sat upon the bow of a boat while my heart sang a carol of joy at the rush of white water below me, the sail's graceful curve against the blue sky, the long wake inscribed by a creature to whom the wind gave purpose and the breath of life. Beauty and joy are precious gifts, and I have found them often on the bow of a sailboat.

The Melville Whaling Room of the New Bedford Free Public Library houses some 95,000 items of manuscript and printed materials, including more than 500 ship's logs. Its dedicated curator until his death early in 1973 was Reginald B. Hegarty, a spare little man with the merriness of youth still in him.

"I retired from whaling at the age of 11," he was fond of saying, and it was the truth.

"I went to sea at one and a half years of age," he told me. "My parents took a baby carriage along and bolted it to the deck of the brig *Sullivan*. That was my father's vessel; he was her captain and one-third owner." Mr. Hegarty didn't remember much about his first two expeditions on the *Sullivan*, but he had good recall of his third and final voyage, aboard the *Alice Knowles*.

Did he ever go out in one of the ship's boats for the actual killing of a whale?

"Yes, but just once," he said. "My father let my brother and me go in one of the boats when it lanced a blackfish, or pilot whale. It was a routine kill, not much incident or danger. But the minute we got back aboard the ship, my mother walloped the whey out of us. She said to my father, 'Can't they get into enough mischief without you helping them?' "

Mr. Hegarty's father was lost aboard the *Alice Knowles* on September 13, 1917, off Cape Hatteras. "After that my mother asked my brother and me not to go back to sea," the curator said, "and we never did."

*F*rom New Bedford, our first foray took us southeasterly across Buzzards Bay toward Massachusetts' offshore isles: Cuttyhunk and the other Elizabeth Islands, and Martha's Vineyard and Nantucket. These lie in some of the most popular of northern cruising grounds, and the water is often alive with sails. But there is frustration for mariners here: Some areas are fogged in 90 days a year, with summer the worst time. Fog is particularly bad in Buzzards Bay itself, and the prevailing summer sou'wester can kick up an annoying sea against an ebb tide.

We found *Andromeda* quite capable at this kind of blue-water slogging, a husky antagonist for rough water, and her stability gave us confidence. Her broad stern sometimes caught steep following waves, giving the helmsman a workout to keep her on course, but we never felt in danger of broaching.

Islands often result in constricted channels where the tides race, and this is particularly true of the rocky approach to Woods Hole; there currents reach five knots. But whenever strong tidal flows caught us near docks or in narrow passages, our diesel overpowered them.

Woods Hole lies at the southwestern tip of Cape Cod, where the land juts out close to the Elizabeth Islands and forms a natural gateway between Buzzards Bay and Vineyard Sound. So the village becomes almost an inevitable port of call for those sailing the offshore isles. I found it doubly interesting: first, as a crowded little maritime crossroads and the port for ferryboats to Martha's Vineyard and Nantucket, and second, as the home of the renowned Woods Hole Oceanographic Institution.

Michael Schofield, a member of the staff, took me to the dock area for a look at a small pilot experiment: a series of tanks containing treated, diluted sewage water, algae, and oysters. That's all—and it took me a moment to grasp its purpose.

Treated sewage often is so rich in nutrients that it triggers an explosive growth of algae when dumped into confined waters. These algae may take from the water too much dissolved oxygen, killing fish and other aquatic creatures, Schofield explained. But shellfish love algae; so the experiment uses treated effluent diluted with sea water as a culture medium for algae. Shellfish not only dine on the algae but remove such products of sewage decomposition as ammonia and phosphate.

Shellfish can concentrate bacteria, viruses, and undesirable chemicals in their meat, yet the research team has used effluent from many different sources without detectable toxic effects.

"If our studies work out, it should be possible to devise a system that could take treated sewage from a city of 50,000 and produce more than 900 tons of oyster meat a year," said Dr. John Ryther, head of the project.

Sewage pollutes many shellfish beds along the Intracoastal Waterway. Perhaps one day some of the little towns we came to know will revitalize their fisheries by aquaculture, while helping clean up the waters at their doors.

*W*halers once worked out of Woods Hole, and they docked where the oceanographic institution now stands. Many of the crewmen were Gay Head Indians from Martha's Vineyard; they had hunted whales in coastal waters long before the coming of the white man. For many years—until his death in 1973 at the age of 88—the Indian patriarch Napoleon Bonaparte Madison was one of only two surviving Vineyard whalemen. To keep a rendezvous with him I journeyed to the island's southwestern end, site of an Indian community atop the multicolored Gay Head cliffs.

Napoleon Madison had a remarkable face, as weathered as the eroded cliffs he had known from childhood. "I was 18 when I started whaling," he recalled. "I shipped out in September 1905 aboard the bark *Josephine*, and just made one voyage of 25 months. I don't remember how I got to be a harpooner. I guess they figured Indians could handle spears well, so why not harpoons? In all, I struck about six whales.

"There were always six men in a whaleboat. Sometimes we sailed; other times we all rowed except the mate, who steered. I pulled the harpooner's oar, and after I struck the whale it was the mate's job to go forward and lance it, for the kill. To harpoon a right whale, you took the boat across his back, from side to side, but with a sperm whale you approached sideways toward the head, then moved down toward the tail."

The old man had been speaking in a quiet, matter-of-fact voice. Now he paused, and when he resumed, his voice took on a vibrant, youthful quality. He switched to the present tense; his hand clenched into a fist on the tabletop between us. Suddenly he was young again, and battling a whale.

"I try to hit six to eight inches behind the spout hole," he said. "When I strike, the mate comes forward. He knows when to cut the line to the harpoon if the whale sounds and pulls us under. The whale runs to windward, always, sometimes for miles, and it can be three hours or three days before the ship comes. But you keep hauling on the line; you pull closer and closer until the mate lances the whale. Now, maybe a stove boat, like that other time. If it happens . . . aaah, the cold! You cling to the wreckage until another boat picks you up. You don't feel the chill so much in the water. It's the air—the cold that hits you as soon as they pull you out." *(Continued on page 38)*

Narrow spits of land connect the pieces of Cuttyhunk Island, westernmost of the Elizabeth chain. Nestled in the crook of Copicut Neck, the island's northern peninsula, Cuttyhunk Pond provides a deep, sheltered anchorage for fishing boats and visiting yachts. Below, Mystic Whaler—a ghost ship in the early morning fog—moves slowly out of the Pond after weighing anchor. Copied from a famous 19th-century whaling schooner, the vessel makes spring and summer excursions along the Atlantic Coast.

Village of Cuttyhunk, overlooking the Pond, survives on summer seafaring activity. Stopping overnight on an American Yacht Club cruise, Bruce Smart (below, at left), his wife, Edie (in striped shirt), and their crew on the March Hare *cook freshly caught striped bass for dinner. At times more than 200 boats crowd into Cuttyhunk Pond, a virtually landlocked harbor with good guest-yacht facilities. A friendly deer (opposite, below), startled by a stranger, bounds away to safety. A large herd of deer roams the island, and many of the animals venture into the village at night to browse on shrubs and sample unprotected gardens. Island regulations prohibit hunting, and residents vigorously discourage poachers.*

Sports fisherman Justin Burns wheels his catch of striped bass past lobster traps on Fisherman's Dock at Cuttyhunk. Well known as a fertile fishing ground, the island once served as the almost exclusive province of a sportsmen's club. Today fishing guides catering to the public operate charter boats from the dock. A symbolic striped bass swings freely atop the town's one church, which is shared by three denominations. A summer newsboy (below) hawks morning papers brought by the daily airplane from New Bedford, 14 miles away. The marina plays an important role in the village economy; dockage fees, collected daily by the wharfinger, or dock manager, make up much of the municipal revenue.

He stopped, and took his eyes from the sea. The magic moment was over. Napoleon Madison was once again an old man.

I met the former harpooner through his friends Capt. and Mrs. Donald Le Mar Poole, of Menemsha, devoted natives of the island who live in a sturdy, shingled dwelling on a little knoll overlooking a sheltered backwater. For nearly all his 69 years Donald Poole has been a lobsterman; he began by helping his father when he was 7, and he still maintains 260 lobster pots, pulling up and emptying 75 to 100 of them each day. It's hard physical labor, but there are many such older men at work along the Waterway, from oystermen of the Chesapeake to seiners in Virginia and the Carolinas and shrimpers in Georgia and Florida. The water is the only life they know or want to know, and they hold to it as long as they can.

"My ancestors came here in 1642," says Captain Poole, a burly man of easy smiles whose relaxed air is enhanced by the old pipe he rarely puts down. "Ever since then, none of us has been able to raise enough money to get off the island." That is a favorite joke; the captain's circumstances are quite comfortable. Nor would he ever leave. He often refers to his island as a place happily divorced from the mainland. "What have you got in America that we need?" he asks.

Then he looks out upon sea and sky and marsh, his mood turns serious, and he adds, "We have deep roots here. This very land where our house sits was planted in corn by my great-great-great-grandfather. My wife is the ninth generation of her family on Martha's Vineyard. Our son is the tenth, his children the eleventh. There is continuity here."

The professional watermen I have met do not pursue that way of life just for the money. The water is not only their life but their love, and from it they draw a serenity denied most men.

"You leave your problems on the breakwater when you go out," said Captain Poole. "They're waiting for you when you get back, but somehow they look smaller. The change lies in yourself. You've found something out there, a kind of renewal."

*T*wo days later I thought of the captain as *Andromeda* powered through windless seas en route to Newport, Rhode Island. Rain seemed imminent, and as we drew abeam of Butter Ball Rock off Newport Neck, I was tempted to increase speed and get into port as quickly as possible. But then I recalled Poole's Law: "You're only going to find more trouble sooner if you get there quicker." This sensibly languid view of travel by boat persuaded me to dawdle; and I was glad I did, for only ten minutes later both wind and sun rejoined us, and blithe little waves shattered the rays of light into myriad, gleaming fragments.

Our renewed wind blew from the southwest, the prevailing quarter in summertime, and suggested insistently that we set the genoa for a nice run into the harbor. So the sail billowed out from its neat roller furl, and, after killing the engine, we moved along in blessed quiet at the respectable speed of four knots.

Newport's waters, like those of New Bedford, bring many a historic image to mind. Here we sailed in the wake of laden barks and brigs that plied colonial America's profitable "triangle trade": rum to Africa, slaves to the West Indies, molasses to New England. Here we followed the track of a British invasion fleet that occupied Newport in 1776 and remained nearly three years. Here, too, we shared the sea with the ghosts of the great steam yachts from Newport's gilded era at the turn of the century, Vincent Astor's *Nourmahal* and J. P. Morgan's *Corsair*.

To this day Newport retains its unofficial title as the nation's yachting capital. The America's Cup Race is sailed offshore from the harbor, and yachting's elite gather for the Newport-Bermuda and Annapolis-Newport races.

We passed between Fort Adams and Goat Island and sailed slowly past the Ida Lewis Yacht Club at the entrance to the inner harbor. The famous club stands on a rock well offshore, and a long pier now links it to the land. But a lighthouse once occupied the site, and there Ida Lewis, like her father before her, served as keeper. During a long life on the rock that remarkable woman, a strong swimmer and excellent boat handler, saved 23 people from drowning in Newport waters. She died a national heroine in 1911.

Newport's waterfront is an intriguing jumble of old commercial docks, boatyards, marinas, and warehouses extending along shoreside Thames Street. Goat Island, once owned by the Navy but now the site of a hotel and marina, forms a protective barrier on the other side of the harbor. Masts towering above the waterfront drew us to the harbor's head. There we idled offshore for a long, appreciative look at the 125-foot topsail schooner *Bill of Rights,* tied up at her dock awaiting a new group of charter passengers. To the north, at Goat Island Causeway, we could see a replica of the British frigate H.M.S. *Rose,* which blockaded Newport during the Revolutionary War.

The sun scattered the last remnants of clouds as *Andromeda* entered a marina along the oldest part of the waterfront.

The wealthiest families in America made Newport their summer playground at the turn of the century, and some still do. Along Bellevue Avenue, and atop rocky coves overlooking the sea from Ocean Drive and Cliff Walk, these families built fabulous mansions they called "summer cottages."

Time and taxes exacted their toll, and eventually five of the largest and most elegant houses passed into the sympathetic hands of the Preservation Society of Newport County. It now owns and keeps open for public viewing The Breakers, Marble House, The Elms, Chateau-sur-Mer, and Rosecliff.

Among these grandiose monuments to another time, The Breakers, completed in 1895 for Cornelius Vanderbilt, is often acclaimed the most magnificent. Its formal rooms on the first floor contain an extraordinary display of treasures, from huge

Overleaf: Lifelines awash, Jubilee III *heels over in a stiff southwest breeze shortly after the start of the 1972 Newport-to-Bermuda Race. The 73-foot ketch, owned by the U. S. Naval Academy, completed the 635-mile course in about three and a half days. Gale-force winds and high seas battered the fleet during the race, leaving only a few of the 178 starters undamaged at the finish.*

crystal chandeliers to a stained glass skylight, from paintings by old masters to exquisite tapestries.

But the loveliest mansion by far—in Mike's and my opinion—is Rosecliff, designed by Stanford White for Mrs. Hermann Oelrichs as an evocation of the two Trianons at Versailles.

Every year the Newport Music Festival stages programs in the glittering settings of the mansions, and Mike, Bill, and I thoroughly enjoyed a concert of Spanish chamber music at Rosecliff. We couldn't find seats in the crowded ballroom, so we listened from perches on the grand staircase, feeling like bleacherites at a ball game until we became absorbed in the music.

*A*nother organization, the Newport Restoration Foundation, is sometimes confused with the Preservation Society but has a different aim and method of operating. The foundation acquires 17th- and 18th-century houses and painstakingly restores them, then rents them as private residences.

Its director, architect F. A. Comstock, said the foundation now owns 60 old homes, including 25 that have been fully restored. He took me to see one of them, a delightful little house at 18 Thames Street, part of which was built in 1670. Inside it was all lilliputian charm but, understandably, a bit out of plumb.

Redevelopment of Newport's commercial district also has been pushed vigorously, notably at Bowen's Wharf, where a company headed by 34-year-old Bart Dunbar has restored a number of 18th- and 19th-century buildings and put up some new ones whose design is in keeping with the setting.

During a succession of soft summer evenings we lounged in *Andromeda*'s cockpit, lazily enjoying the sights and sounds of the busy port. A number of sailboats that had recently finished the Single-handed Transatlantic Race lay at the marina adjoining our own. Their skippers kept up a daily round of visits and parties—survival euphoria, perhaps, for an Atlantic storm had damaged several of the boats.

On our last evening in Newport, we had just finished a leisurely dinner in *Andromeda*'s cockpit when Bill exclaimed: "Fire! There, in that old building on Thames Street!"

He pointed. Black smoke poured from the windows, and flame flickered red inside. The structure, built about 1750, had been undergoing renovation preparatory to being moved to another site. Marina partying came to a sober halt, and hundreds of boatmen watched while firemen fought to save the old tinderbox.

And they did save it. Flames damaged the interior, but the sturdy walls remained virtually unscathed.

We sailed the next morning, and as we left the dock I looked back at the damaged building, a house older than our nation, and rejoiced that it still stood, blackened but triumphant. Like so many other remarkable structures, it would enjoy a resurrection in Newport, a community that lives with equal zest in the past and in the present.

Newport mansions along Cliff Walk sparkle in the late afternoon sun. The Breakers (middleground), built as a summer residence for Cornelius Vanderbilt in 1893-95, symbolizes an opulent era when Newport attracted America's leading architects and landscape designers. Scenic three-mile Cliff Walk, once a fishermen's path, meanders along the rocky shore; it remains open to the public by state law.

2

Long Island Sound: The Boatmen's Boulevard

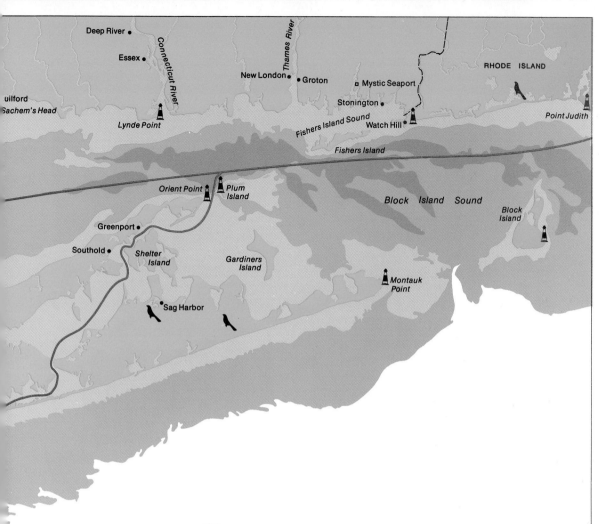

The map labels, reading across the image, include:

Deep River •   Essex •   New London •   Groton   Mystic Seaport   RHODE ISLAND

Connecticut River   Thames River

Guilford   Sachem's Head   Stonington •

Lynde Point   Fishers Island Sound   Watch Hill •   Point Judith

Fishers Island

Orient Point •   Plum Island   Block Island Sound   Block Island

Greenport •   Southold •   Shelter Island   Gardiners Island

Sag Harbor   Montauk Point

The main Waterway route passes through busy Long Island Sound, paralleling New York and Connecticut shores. An alternate course weaves between Long Island and its barrier beaches.

G ray sea . . . gray overcast, with the sun never quite cutting through . . . a soft, ineffectual breeze from all over the compass. Off our starboard beam I could see Point Judith, Rhode Island, a sandy nose wide open to the pounding of the sea—but exposed to as complacent an Atlantic as I had ever seen.

Neither very high nor very rugged, Point Judith didn't appear to deserve its fearsome reputation. But the rocky shoals at its base claimed many an old windjammer, and we looked soberly at three massive stone breakwaters built by the Corps of Engineers as a harbor of refuge.

From Judith's tip rose an octagonal stone lighthouse, a landmark since 1816, and beneath it we could glimpse the white buildings of a Coast Guard station. Lookouts kept watch from the same spot in colonial days for ships in trouble.

Let me confess that I am not a purist about sailing. If the air is light and vagrant, if I am trying to keep a schedule, I will "hoist the iron sail"—turn on the engine—and I did so now.

Light air does offer one advantage: ease of eating. On a windy day years ago, when Mike and I were new to sailing, she prepared for lunch a delicious but drippy hamburger sandwich called a Sloppy Joe. Four of us tried to eat this aptly named concoction while the boat heeled and bucked in a stiff head sea. If we had deliberately thrown our food at one another, the mess

in the cockpit could not have been worse. From that moment on, we ruled out anything messy for lunch, except in light air. So now Mike went below to fire up the oven for open-face sandwiches: toast with melted cheese topped by slices of tomato and bacon—fiendishly slippery in an active sea.

While Mike cooked and Bill steered, I read to them an appropriate passage from *The Boy, Me and the Cat.* On October 18, 1912, little *Mascot* passed Point Judith under sail and the Plummers cooked a hot lunch on their coal stove, with near dire results for the cat, Scotty. *Mascot*'s log tells the tale:

"Beautiful day with easy sea and crew engaged in ship's duties and sewing launch fender. Some little hubble-bubble outside and coot stew slopped over on Scotty but did not scald her. Later while asleep in her basket the beans came flying to leeward. She heard them on their way and escaped from under by a flying leap to cockpit. Quite a day for Scotty."

*P*redictably, Bill Gay glimpsed the 61-foot light and horn atop Watch Hill Point before I did. Bill always picked up navigational aids two or three minutes ahead of me, and we were grateful many times for the acuity of those young eyes. *Andromeda* slipped through Watch Hill Passage, left Sugar Reef and Catumb Rocks behind, and powered down Fishers Island Sound with a long succession of rocks to port—their jagged black tops sometimes exposed or awash—and Latimer Reef to starboard. In this one area we threaded our way through more rocks and reefs than we would see anywhere else on the entire Waterway. But the well-marked sound presented no problem in good visibility, and soon Ram Island lay abeam and we were off the entrance to Mystic Harbor and Mystic River.

Here again, with plentiful navigation markers and no fog, a path through rocks and shoals proved easy for a boat under power. But I could appreciate how difficult the narrow, tortuous passage would be in poor visibility—and the problem it presented in the Age of Sail. Mystic built stout ships from the earliest colonial days: at first, coastal trading sloops and schooners, then sealers and whalers that penetrated the Antarctic, and tall clippers that stormed around Cape Horn and became the glory of all the world's seas. How impatiently captains must have awaited favorable winds or tides to get out of Mystic!

Like so many New England villages once famed for shipbuilding, Mystic's fortunes declined with the slow passing of wooden ships and iron men; finally the community's seafaring tradition itself seemed in danger of death by neglect. Then, in 1929, three residents founded the Marine Historical Association. Beginning with one building and a small collection, the museum has grown to more than 60 buildings and exhibits, and numerous ships and small craft.

This is Mystic Seaport, where many hands and minds have fashioned a representative New England maritime town of the

Surging under full canvas before a stiff wind, the U. S. Coast Guard's three-masted bark Eagle *provides cadets with some challenging training—and a direct link with the timeless traditions of seafaring.*

Overleaf: A Coast Guard Academy crew carries out the precarious task of a "harbor furl." As the Eagle *heads into its New London home, the phrase "taut ship" takes on vivid reality for safety-belted cadets straining to fold a mainsail along the yardarm.*

19th century. It is a living museum, not a static display. We encountered that fact before we even docked, when an old whaleboat filled with youthful rowers crossed our stern. Athletic-looking boys manned all the oars, but the person at the tiller was unmistakably a girl.

They were part of what Waldo C. M. Johnston, Mystic Seaport's director, calls his MOD Squad: Mystic Orientation Demonstration. While visitors watched and applauded, they demonstrated boat handling, conducted sail drill high in the rigging of the training ship *Joseph Conrad,* and imparted to the cobbled waterfront an air of purposeful bustle as they spliced line, built lobster traps, and conducted breeches-buoy drills.

Andromeda docked in distinguished company, assigned a berth behind the last of the wooden whalers, *Charles W. Morgan.* We had scarcely made fast our lines when I heard a male voice lifted in an old song somewhere ashore.

"A chanteyman!" I exclaimed, and bolted down the dock. A chanteyman, sweet singer of old work songs! Many years ago most merchant sailing vessels employed one, a man who sang to give sailors the rhythm for performing such team tasks as weighing anchor, hoisting sail, trimming the sheets.

Near the shipsmith shop I found a knot of appreciative listeners around the owner of the voice, 24-year-old Stuart Frank, who teaches philosophy at the University of Bridgeport.

"Mystic Seaport is good at presenting the look and smell of the sea; I thought maybe I could help with the noise," he told me. His noise consisted of many an authentic chantey, sung in a light baritone to concertina accompaniment.

"A lot of these songs are of Anglo-Scots-Irish origin, especially Irish, and many derive from work songs of the black South," Stuart said. "Most were sung without accompaniment, but concertinas or fiddles were sometimes used."

To a rapt audience Stuart sang various kinds of chanteys: a spirited rhythm for hauling on the halyards that mastheaded the yards; slower, more deliberate tempos for heaving the capstan that brought the anchor aboard.

When I asked Stuart for his favorite, he sang "Lowlands," a capstan chantey, unhurried in pace and hauntingly beautiful:

I had a dream the other night
Lowlands, lowlands,   Away my John.
I dreamt my love came home from sea
My lowlands away.
I'll never return to you, he said,
Lowlands, lowlands,   Away my John.
The briny tide washes o'er my head
My lowlands away.

As the chanteyman sang he wove a spell, and when he finished the listeners paid him the compliment of a long, reflective moment before applauding.

When we wanted to know more about anything we saw,

"interpreters" were promptly at hand. In the shops, craftsmen —woodworker, shipsmith, weaver, printer—demonstrated their skills and patiently explained the old techniques.

The smith, Emil Johnson, 82 years old but still powerfully built and straight as a well-forged harpoon, enjoyed an audience that included many children. One boy of about 10 was working the bellows at the forge to heat the end of a thin metal rod. Mr. Johnson showed him how to pound the glowing metal into the shape of a rough but serviceable nail. Leaving, the boy proudly clutched his handiwork.

*T*he *Morgan*, that rugged old veteran of 37 long whaling expeditions and 80 years of active service, ranks as the Seaport's premier exhibit. Built in New Bedford in 1841, she took aboard the blubber and bone of 2,000 whales in her day, and outlived all her contemporaries. The Marine Historical Association acquired her in her centenary year. After more than three decades of resting on a sand and gravel berth at her dock, she will soon be refloated and hauled for hull repairs as part of her restoration.

As I walked the *Morgan*'s decks, I marveled at how much equipment and how many men could be crammed aboard a vessel of only 113 feet. On her foredeck she still carries the big brick firepit and two huge pots known as the tryworks. Here the oil was cooked from thick slices of blubber called bible leaves; when it cooled, the oil drained off into barrels stored deep in the hold. This process went on for hours while flensers, working from a platform rigged outboard and amidships, cut and peeled the skin and oil-rich blubber from the whale's immense carcass as it floated alongside the ship.

I tried to imagine the stench. Napoleon Madison, the old Indian harpooner at Gay Head, had said:

"I can't describe the odor; it was sickening, and you were never really free of it. After a kill we'd clean up the ship, and the sea air on deck would clear your head some, but the smell from the barrels and whalebone stowed below was always there, and the smell was always in your clothes. When you met other people ashore, they could hardly stand it."

The *Morgan* carried 33 officers and men. The officers shared tiny cabins in the stern—except the captain, who had a day cabin and a stateroom equipped (because one captain's wife had accompanied him) with a handsome double bed. The crew's cramped quarters were in the forecastle below decks. I could visualize the 20 bunks it once contained, and the crewmen bending over as they moved about, for no one of average height could have stood upright.

Grasping the wheel of another old marvel, the full-rigged *Joseph Conrad*, I imagined I could hear the Australian accent of Capt. Alan Villiers as he hurled orders to the crew of venturesome youths who took the *Conrad* on a 58,000-mile voyage

*Dawn illumines the still waters of Mystic Seaport, the maritime museum
at Mystic, Connecticut. The village rose to prominence and prosperity
in the early years of the 19th century on the high tide of Yankee sealing,
whaling, and shipbuilding. Today, near the yards that once launched
swift clipper ships, the living museum displays representative examples
of 19th-century crafts and industries, a dozen historic sailing vessels, and
more than a hundred smaller craft. The 103-foot* Joseph Conrad
*(background) served as a Danish merchant training vessel from 1882
until 1934, then made a 58,000-mile circuit of the world. It retired to
its present berth in 1947. At left, a Mystic Seaport crew that includes
Kathy Monohan and Bob Francis provides a whaleboat demonstration.*

Mystic Seaport ship carver Willard Shepard shapes from glued pine planks a grape-ornamented seal (opposite) for the Old Connecticut Statehouse at Hartford. Eagles, figureheads, and sternboards emerge from the fragrant chips and shavings as Shepard demonstrates a distinctive craft of New England's maritime heyday. The ship chandlery (left) stocks oars, kegs for salted fish, drawers of brass hardware—reminiscent of the dockside general store that could supply everything from rum to oilskins.

around the world in the 1930's. At the museum, which has owned her since 1947, she is used to teach basic maritime skills to boys and girls enrolled in mariner training programs. Now, however, the venerable *Conrad* never knows the scend of the sea beneath her keel; she stays at her dock.

On our last night I watched the fog roll in, and as darkness fell the mist seemed to invite old ghosts to walk the Seaport, and later enhanced the antique appeal of narrow streets and early-American homes as we drove through nearby Stonington.

*R*ain clouds seemed to clot above our heads as we left Mystic next day, but the sun finally won the morning's battle. *Andromeda*'s crew watched the contest from Fishers Island Sound, cheering for the sun. But later Bill and I rigged the white nylon sunshade that suspends from the main boom like a tent to protect the cockpit. We can't use the mainsail with the shade in place, but when it's hot enough we don't care. We lolled contentedly in the cockpit and cruised under power.

Skirting those rotund islets called North Dumpling and South Dumpling, we entered West Harbor at Fishers Island. The pirate Captain Kidd supposedly buried some of his loot near Treasure Pond and Money Pond on the 12-mile-long island. At its nearest point to the mainland it lies only two miles off the Connecticut coast, and by geographic logic it should be a part of Connecticut; but in fact it remains a part of the town of Southold in Suffolk County, New York, 18 miles away at the northeastern end of Long Island.

I expected to find palaces such as those along Newport's Ocean Drive, but none loomed anywhere on the island's pleasantly rural horizon. We saw some good but modest homes, and I applauded the potholed state of the one paved road, deliberately left in disrepair to discourage speeding motorcars.

A brief run, again in hot, humid weather, brought *Andromeda* to "The Port." That's what natives of New London, Connecticut, call their harbor, one of the state's busiest and biggest, home of the U. S. Coast Guard Academy and, on the Groton side of the Thames River, the huge U. S. Naval Submarine Base. The 1,100-acre installation, bordered by a string of 15 piers stretching nearly a mile and a half along the river, contains more than 230 buildings, including new complexes for the Naval Submarine School and the Submarine Medical Center.

A mammoth new pier was under construction, and others were being modified to take the big nuclear-powered attack and missile submarines.

Impressive, yes; but the noisy industrial facilities of the base did not interest me as much as the little marina I found on a relatively quiet part of the Navy's waterfront. Seventy small boats lay at their berths, some for rent to station personnel, others owned by members of the Navy Sailing Association.

Downstream on the other side of the river the Coast Guard

Academy, with its manicured lawns and red brick Georgian architecture, looked as handsome as any small New England college. My visit came on the eve of Parents Day, and all cadets not in class seemed to be down on the athletic field helping set up for a big picnic and barbecue.

Coast Guard cadets win admission on the basis of competitive examinations, not Congressional appointments. No rigidly prescribed course of study confronts these talented youngsters. Capt. Paul F. Foye, the academic dean, explained to me that after the first year a cadet may specialize in any of 13 academic options. He acquires many of his maritime skills on summer cruises aboard Coast Guard vessels, including that splendid anachronism, the three-masted training bark *Eagle*.

*F*rom New London we cruised leisurely down the Connecticut coast, pondering the vagabond's carefree question: Where next? We had heard many good things about the Connecticut River, so after a series of easy tacks into a light wind, we entered its channel.

The Connecticut proved a delightful contrast to the industrial hodgepodge and restive waters of New London. Once past the powerplant and two bridges near the river's mouth, we moved upstream by restful, wooded shores and solitary homes. With growing pleasure we entered the picturesque stretch leading to Essex, took a lingering and appreciative look at the town itself, then put into Essex Island Marina.

The heart of the town lies atop a hill above the harbor, and tree-shaded streets run down to the water. We saw many fine old frame houses meticulously kept; some bore plaques with 18th-century dates of construction. The waterfront is a pleasant, salty assortment of boatyards, marinas, and restaurants.

About a mile and a half west of the river is the old frame station of the Valley Railroad Company. In 1968 antique railroad buffs decided to recondition a short but scenic stretch of abandoned track along the Connecticut River. They acquired and restored some venerable coaches and other rolling stock, including three steam engines, notably "Old 103" of the Sumpter and Choctaw Railroad. Now the buffs run their train several times daily in summer between Essex and Deep River, through woodland and along panoramic reaches of unspoiled river.

Bill Gay is too young to remember steam trains, but what memories "Old 103" brought back to Mike and me! The wail of a steam whistle—how well I could remember hearing that mournful sound in the nights of my childhood. I grew up in the railroad town of Cumberland, Maryland, where our evening entertainment often consisted of going down to the station to watch the Capital Limited roll in; it stopped three minutes before chuffing off to such places of high mystery as Pittsburgh and Chicago. Now, aboard this charming relic of the past, I closed my eyes to the scenery and just listened.

En route back to Essex, a wind shift swept some coal smoke into our coach, and on the nearest window we could hear a soft telltale whispering, like sleet against the glass.

"Listen! Do you hear that?" Bill asked excitedly. "That must be cinders!"

"Yes, real cinders," I agreed nostalgically, wiping one from my right eye.

Any port of call after Essex has to be a comedown, I thought the next day as we set a southwesterly course down the Sound.

How wrong I was! Off Sachem's Head we kept well clear of two nun buoys marking a group of malevolent-looking rocks, then turned and slipped into a compact, rock-girt harbor.

One monolith, an island unto itself with a footbridge to the mainland, served as foundation for the Sachem's Head Yacht Club, a weathered frame building that looked as if it had grown from the granite. Around the harbor's perimeter houses perched atop the stony outcrops, and on the sparkling water moored sailboats made obeisance as wavelets played under their bows.

We took a mooring, piled into our inflatable rubber dinghy, and set a winding course through the fleet for the shoreside home of Milton Bullard. Mr. Bullard, who had just retired as First Selectman of Guilford, of which Sachem's Head is a part, had hospitably agreed to introduce us to some of his neighbors before taking us to the yacht club for a picnic dinner. Soon we were deep in conversation with a roomful of friendly people.

"I was born and raised in Maine," said businessman Leighton Lee, "and this harbor is the nearest spot to Maine in appearance that I could find. I wanted rocks, a deep harbor, a protected cove. Do I sail? You might as well ask if I breathe!"

I asked about the name Sachem's Head, and our host had the answer. Two years before the settlement of Guilford in 1639, two Indian tribes fought a bloody battle nearby. The victors beheaded the defeated sachem, or chief, and placed his head in an oak tree—a grisly lookout staring off into the Sound.

Sachem's Head harbor does have one conspicuous fault; it lies open to the west. All night *Andromeda* pitched and rolled at her mooring, and her crew got little sleep. The day dawned gray, with low clouds scudding along before a stiff southwest wind, and the radio's weatherman promised worsening conditions

Andromeda heads south along the Inland Waterway with her skipper, Allan Fisher, at the wheel. The author's wife, Mike, who signed on for the voyage as "chief cook and counselor," emerges from the motorsailer's spacious aft cabin.

by nightfall. In rough seas we got under way for New Haven.

Just west of Sachem's Head the Thimble Islands lie scattered in a craggy maze. There are dozens of these outcroppings, and in good weather we would have enjoyed cruising among them, for they are separated by deep channels. But the southwest wind hurled some nasty seas at our bow, and we took aboard sheets of chill spray. No one expressed regret as we bade goodbye to the Sound and motored inside the breakwaters shielding New Haven harbor.

That port, like New London, is big and commercial, and New Haven itself is heavily industrial. But New Haven also has Yale University, as it has since 1716, a sufficiently redeeming factor for almost any visitor.

Professor Eric Mood, whose specialty is environmental health, serves as adviser to the New England River Basins Commission, now conducting a study of the Sound that will result in a comprehensive plan for protecting, developing, and using it. Not counting New York City, more than 2,500,000 people live in communities adjoining the Sound, and 60 municipal and institutional systems discharge sewage and waste water into it. Eighteen electric power plants dump heated water. More than 50 per cent of the Sound's marshlands have been destroyed.

I called upon Professor Mood at his office in a tall building that stands only 500 yards from where the first New Haven settlers landed in 1636. Picking up a pamphlet, he waved it and said, "This is a publication issued in 1918; it discusses the sewage disposal problem of New Haven. Not much has changed for the better since then. Furthermore, the closer you get to New York City, the worse the problem. Nearly all disposal plants provide at least primary treatment, but there are some communities in New York that dump raw sewage into the Sound."

But he spoke optimistically about the impact of the forthcoming study report. "Hopefully it will bring some sense of order to what we are doing," he said. "Overall planning is badly needed. After the year 2000 we will have only two choices in the Long Island Sound area: We will either use recycled water or desalinated water. But at this point a lot of people are not ready to accept either one."

The Sound contains some 227,000 registered boats, and they add up to plenty of work for the Coast Guard's Group Long Island Sound, with headquarters on the New Haven waterfront. When I visited the installation, I was amazed at how much is done for so many by so few. The group consists of only 200 regular Coast Guardsmen, and it has only 15 patrol vessels to cover the entire Sound. Yet in a year's time its communications network handles some 4,100 distress calls. Guardsmen themselves respond to 1,600 of those calls, the various state marine police handle about 1,500, and the Coast Guard Auxiliary takes care of the rest.

The auxiliary is particularly active along the heavily traveled

Intracoastal Waterway. "They provide my group with 15 to 20 boats and crews each weekend," said Capt. J. L. Fleishel. "Members of the auxiliary get no pay, just their expenses, and not nearly enough credit. Many make sacrifices to serve. Without them I don't think we could perform our mission."

When we left New Haven the weather again put on a benign face, and we enjoyed a leisurely cruise to Milford. Mike took a nap, I daydreamed, and Bill slumped back in the helmsman's seat and manipulated the wheel with his bare feet.

Milford, on the Wepawaug River, enjoys a high reputation among yachtsmen, but the river everywhere is quite narrow. So many boats crowded those waters that we felt like a log caught in a jam.

But the very first glimpse of Stratford on the broader Housatonic pleased all three of us. As we approached the town from a northerly bend of the river, we saw a huge gray frame building surrounded by bright flags and topped by a jaunty little cupola. It was the American Shakespeare Festival Theater, a resounding success ever since it opened its doors in 1955. For 12 weeks each summer the theater's repertory company presents — along with other outstanding plays — selected works of the playwright who made that other Stratford so famous.

From the marina it was an easy walk to the theater, and we got there early enough to enjoy the outside show by minstrels in Elizabethan costume who strolled the grounds entertaining scores of picnickers. When the doors opened we went in for a superior performance of *Antony and Cleopatra*. The next day Shaw's *Major Barbara* was on the bill of fare, and that too proved exhilarating theater.

Our next stop was Southport on the narrow Mill River, its channel so crowded with boats I wouldn't have thought one more could wedge in. But the harbor is such a perfect miniature, such an appealing haven, that we accepted the nautical clutter as if it were part of some altogether fitting decor. Handsome homes rise along the shores, and a huge weathered frame building that once was an onion warehouse dominates the inner harbor. Now it is the exclusive Pequot Yacht Club.

Harry Bonner, a tall chap with the slender, fit look of the inveterate sailor, met us, along with an interesting array of his sailing friends. At lunch I particularly enjoyed sitting beside Ernest A. Ratsey, retired chairman of Ratsey & Lapthorn, among the oldest and best known of the world's sailmakers. The firm made many of the sails that carried Nelson to victory at Trafalgar. Mr. Ratsey's son, Colin, whom I had met in St. Petersburg when taking delivery of *Andromeda*, is the sixth generation of his family to serve in the company.

Throughout the luncheon Mr. Ratsey kept me fascinated with his recollections. He sailed aboard 13 of the old "J boats," the huge racing yachts that defended the *(Continued on page 65)*

Playing Elizabethan melodies on recorders, strolling musicians help
set the mood for picnickers and other early arrivals at the American
Shakespeare Festival Theater in Stratford. English settlers established
the Connecticut town—naming it for Stratford-on-Avon—in 1639, only
23 years after Shakespeare's death. Every summer since 1955, enthusiastic audiences have flocked to the big gray playhouse (patterned after
the Globe Theatre of Shakespeare's London) on the banks of the
Housatonic River. There a resident company reinforced with prominent
stage and screen performers recreates at least one tragedy and one
comedy by Shakespeare, along with plays by Shaw, Eliot, and O'Neill.
"A morsel for a monarch," the Queen of the Nile describes herself in
Antony and Cleopatra; Salome Jens (opposite) as the Egyptian ruler
assesses her makeup and awaits her first cue. Between appearances
on stage, a richly costumed player passes the time with a game of chess.

Enticing territory for explorers,
a place of beaches, bird sanctuaries
vacation homes—and perhaps the
site of Captain Kidd's buried gold—
the Norwalk Islands extend
four miles just off the Connecticut
shore. A deserted house on Chimon
Island creaks to the cautious tread
of young visitors from the mainland.
The Sheffield Island lighthouse
(opposite), now a summer home,
once alerted mariners to the
Norwalks' girdle of rocks and shoals.

America's Cup until monetary considerations forced a switch to the smaller 12-meter craft. On one occasion Commodore Harold Vanderbilt, winningest of all the Cup skippers, took a fancy to a genoa jib of a new kind and cut that he had seen while readying his *Enterprise* for competition. Without a word Mr. Ratsey went ashore, worked all night with his sailmakers, and came back early the next morning with the new sail.

"Ernest, you look awful. Where have you been?" the commodore asked suspiciously.

"Making that new jib," said Ernest, "and here it is."

"Already? That's impossible!"

"Not when you say you want it," said Ernest, with quiet satisfaction.

"That's the sort of thing I enjoyed doing," Mr. Ratsey told me. "I liked my work, from the time I began as an apprentice sailmaker until I retired at 70."

So far in our cruise of the Sound, we had put in only at ports along the mainland. But now we wanted to see something of Long Island, and off we sailed on a southeast heading for Port Jefferson and its big, well-protected harbor. At a fuel dock a familiar figure waved us ashore, and we picked up photographer Jim Amos. Out of the harbor we

went in glorious sunny weather. Jim wanted photographs of *Andromeda* under sail, and we put him off in the dinghy to shoot us as we swept majestically by.

So what happened? Any sailor knows the answer. The wind promptly died. Our sails slatted lethargically, and *Andromeda* sat in the water with no more energy than a piece of flotsam.

Chesapeake oystermen who sail the old skipjacks have a superstition about dead calm: If the captain throws a penny overboard, a nice little breeze will spring up. It's called "buying the wind." They tell the story of one captain who, not having a penny, threw a nickel into the bay. Within minutes a gale hit his skipjack. Fighting to pull down his maddened sails, he shouted to a crewman, "I'm right smart thankful I didn't throw that bay a dime."

I looked in my pocket—and found only a nickel! Prudently, I put it back and called Jim aboard for lunch.

That evening we dropped the hook in the Sandhole, an unusual little bay tucked away just inside the entrance to Port Jefferson harbor. Great, towering sand dunes enclose the inlet, and in this nook scores of boats had anchored. Many had put dinghies ashore with passengers who now frolicked up and down the dunes like children in the sandbox of a giant. Jim and Bill soon joined them.

Young oysters thrive in warm water discharged by the electrical power plant at Northport, Long Island. At the Long Island Oyster Farms, Bob Milliken's aquaculture chores include thinning of screen-grown oysters destined to mature in cold Atlantic beds. Seafood remains one of the special pleasures of life on the Sound; above, caterers prepare a traditional clambake at the Norwalk Shore and Country Club.

A middle-aged man sailing a little dinghy crossed *Andromeda*'s stern, and I saw him read her name and hailing port, Annapolis.

He called to me, "Is the food still good at the Little Campus Inn?" I laughed and said, "It sure is—and you're a graduate of the Naval Academy."

He had named an Annapolis restaurant long a favorite of midshipmen and their dates.

"You're right," he responded as the dinghy sailed away, "and I'm retiring to Annapolis next year. I'll be seeing you, *Andromeda*."

Long Island is aptly named; it extends 118 miles, and its "fishtail," the bifurcated eastern end, offers a cruising world all its own. Not even our leisurely schedule permitted an examination by boat of this large area; so I drove to Greenport, took the car ferry to Shelter Island, and then another ferry to Sag Harbor, principal object of my trip. Shelter Island proved woodsy and quiet and reminded me of Fishers Island. Old Sag Harbor turned out to be perhaps the loveliest of all the picturesque ports we had seen.

In 1790 Congress designated Sag Harbor an official port of entry in the same bill that named New York City as such. Of the two, Sag Harbor at that time had more vessels engaged in foreign commerce. For almost a century—from 1775 to 1871—whaling was its principal industry, and the port built many of the ships for that trade. A total of 63 whalers operated out of Sag Harbor in 1845, when the pursuit of Moby Dick was at its peak. The town never forgets its glamorous past, staging each June the annual Old Whaler's Festival.

*I*n dismal, blustery weather that seemed to bite through our foul-weather gear, we took *Andromeda* west on the Sound to Huntington Harbor. All other crowded ports I had entered seemed models of roominess compared to Huntington; hundreds and hundreds of yachts lay at moorings, and clubs and marinas jam-packed with more boats jostled for elbow room along the shores. Chance took us into a marina whose dockmaster had met us in southern waters and recognized *Andromeda*, so we got a berth. He told me Huntington Harbor contained at least 2,000 boats!

Theodore Roosevelt's Victorian home, Sagamore Hill, sits in semi-rural isolation atop Cove Neck at Oyster Bay, near Huntington. The big old dwelling that had sheltered such an active family looked rather as if Teddy had just left it for an African safari. Indeed, the living room still contained an astounding array of trophy heads from animals Roosevelt had shot.

At Kings Point, only 20 miles from New York City, the U. S. Merchant Marine Academy occupies the former estate of Walter P. Chrysler. Here a thousand midshipmen prepare for careers as licensed officers of the United States commercial fleet. Each midshipman serves one year of the four-year course on a merchant ship at sea as an apprentice deck or engine officer.

I spent less time on the campus than I did in one of the academy's fleet of 73 small boats. Some of the midshipmen were racing sailing dinghies in the waters between Kings Point and City Island, and one of their sailing instructors, Michael Gaffney, and I kept an eye on them for a time from a power boat.

*T*he next day, in brilliant sunshine, we sailed back across the Sound from Huntington to the Connecticut shore. Usually, from that part of the Sound, the New York City skyline is either invisible or only a blurry gray suggestion. But during the night, rain and a brisk wind had scoured the atmosphere and we could see the distant skyscrapers, so sharp and clear that it seemed a window between us had been wiped sparkling clean. Weather that fine always lifts a crew's spirits, and we thought *Andromeda* too seemed a bit friskier as she reached toward the mainland. We cruised past Darien, Connecticut, where Mike and I had lived years earlier, and finally tied up at Yacht Haven East, one of the big marinas in the excellent harbor of Stamford.

I wanted to talk to Stamford's mayor, Julius Wilensky, whom the sailing fraternity knows admiringly as a prolific writer for boating magazines and author of three excellent cruising guides —one on Cape Cod waters, one on Long Island Sound, and one on the Windward Islands.

"I don't know very much about the Waterway from Norfolk south," Mr. Wilensky said, "but I have visited every port from Maine to Annapolis, some of them not once but many times. *Pee Gee*, my 22-foot sloop, has poked her bowsprit into all of the 150 harbors we have here on Long Island Sound.

"I'm often asked why I'm so hung up on cruising. I like to explore, to meet new people, to beachcomb. There's a bit of Columbus and Magellan in many of us. And I can say this: I've never been bored sailing. I have enjoyed every cruise I've made; I can't think of a single area I wouldn't go back to."

The mayor gazed from his window onto a busy street as he said this, and there was about him the look and sound of wistful longing for distant ports. We talked for a time about radio direction finders; but as I passed through his door after bidding him goodbye, the mayor was again staring out the window— perhaps seeing *Pee Gee* forging up the Sound hard on the wind, her master at the helm.

Just as we had put into Stamford to see one man, so too did we sail into Larchmont, New York, for the express purpose of spending a day with the legendary Cornelius Shields. He is to sailboat racing what Jack Dempsey is to boxing—a retired elder eminence, his name instantly recognized by any serious follower of the sport. Corny Shields, now 78, twice won the Seawanhaka Cup, internationally regarded as the premier event in small boat racing; he was the first winner of the Mallory Cup, emblematic of the North American sailing championship; and

Cornelius Shields, the "Gray Fox of Long Island Sound," sets out for a sail in his 12-foot-long Tarpon Springs sponge boat, Patience. *Author of the book* Cornelius Shields On Sailing, *and driving force of the venerable Larchmont Yacht Club (background), Corny Shields at 78 exemplifies the best spirit of American yachting. Many times a racing champion, he overcame the effects of a near-fatal heart attack to take the helm of* Columbia *in the tense 1958 final trials of the 12-meter America's Cup competition—and won. As a longtime advocate of one-design racing, in which identical boats and equipment place the burden of winning on the skipper's skills, he inspired a new class of 30-foot racing sloops designed by Olin Stephens. Opposite, colorful spinnakers brighten a Shields-class race among Larchmont Yacht Club enthusiasts.*

he was at the helm of *Columbia,* 1958 America's Cup winner, in its dramatic trial races against *Vim.* He has founded two one-design racing classes, the International and the one that bears his name, the Shields. Through the years he has sailed in some 8,500 races, an incredible record of dedication to a sport.

Larchmont, like Sachem's Head, lay open—in this case to the southwest. But not enough wind blew to raise a ripple as a launch from the Larchmont Yacht Club showed us a guest mooring. Minutes later our dinghy rubbed the club's dock, and our host himself—the "Gray Fox of Long Island Sound," as his sailing opponents long ago dubbed him—helped us ashore.

*M*r. Shields is one of the few elderly men I have met who gives an immediate and strong impression of being much younger than his years. In part it is physical, for he still has the trim and disciplined look of a man who keeps himself in shape for sailing; even more, however, it is his mental outlook. At lunch I found it difficult to get him to talk about the past; instead, he spoke with enthusiasm about the club's junior sailing program, the future of one-design racing, a young man he thought would someday rank with Olin Stephens among the nation's foremost yacht designers. To his speech and thinking he imparted the same verve that had characterized his racing.

"I don't sail competitively now," he said regretfully, "but I love to watch racing. Especially the young people—how I enjoy seeing them develop their skills! Almost every weekend I'm off there in the Sound watching them race, sometimes from the committee boat but often from *Patience.* You did see *Patience,* didn't you?"

Yes, we had seen his boat at her mooring. Cornelius Shields could afford almost any size of sailing vessel; yet his beloved personal yacht is a saucy little 12-foot former sponge boat from Tarpon Springs, Florida, beautifully kept but more than 40 years old. He still sails the tiny thing audaciously around Larchmont, enjoying the fundamental interplay of sail and wind and hull and water as much as he did in his youth.

Corny Shields commissioned Stephens to design the 30-foot racer that now bears the Shields name. So far, more than 200 of the vessels have been built; he paid for most of them, then gave them away to maritime academies, colleges, and universities all over the nation—an action typical of the man.

He saw us off when we returned to *Andromeda.* Gesturing toward the waters off the harbor entrance, he said, "On a weekend, as far east and west as you can see from the middle of the Sound off Larchmont, there are sailboat races. In fact, Corny Jr.'s racing tomorrow. I think I'll sail out and watch the start."

And so we left that youthful man, already planning his next day on the water, a day that would bring him just as much to see and taste and enjoy as any of the golden days aboard *Virginia,* the family sloop he had known as a boy.

Moored boats stud Oyster Bay Harbor like jeweled pins displayed on black velvet. The horseshoe-shaped harbor on Long Island offers many protected anchorages. Large numbers of boats clustered in secluded spots along the shoreline testify to the popularity of sailing on Long Island Sound.

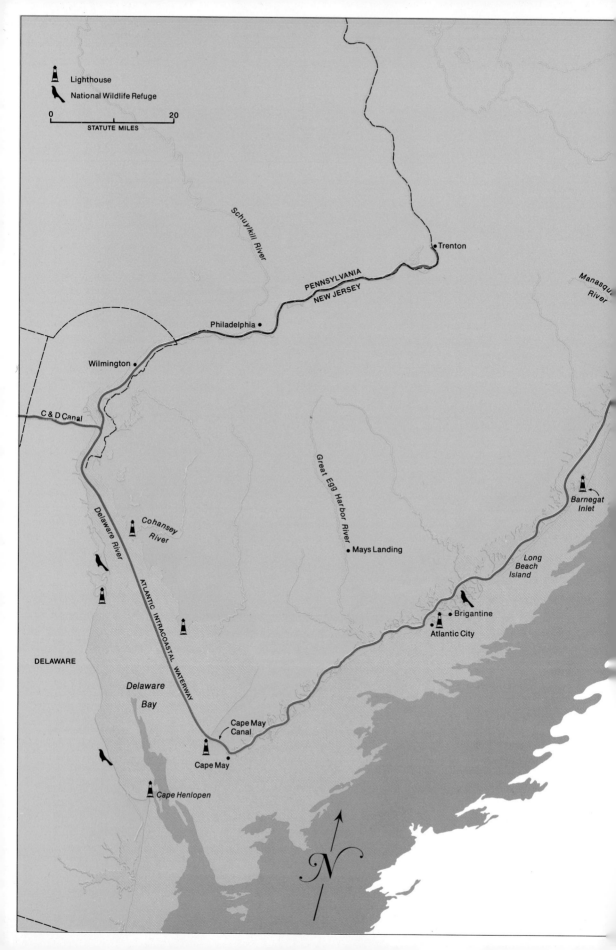

Lighthouse

National Wildlife Refuge

0   20
STATUTE MILES

Schuylkill River

Trenton

PENNSYLVANIA
NEW JERSEY

Manasqu
River

Philadelphia

Wilmington

C & D Canal

Great Egg Harbor River

Barnegat
Inlet

Delaware River

Cohansey
River

Mays Landing

Long
Beach
Island

ATLANTIC INTRACOASTAL WATERWAY

DELAWARE

Brigantine

Atlantic City

Delaware
Bay

Cape May
Canal

Cape May

Cape Henlopen

N

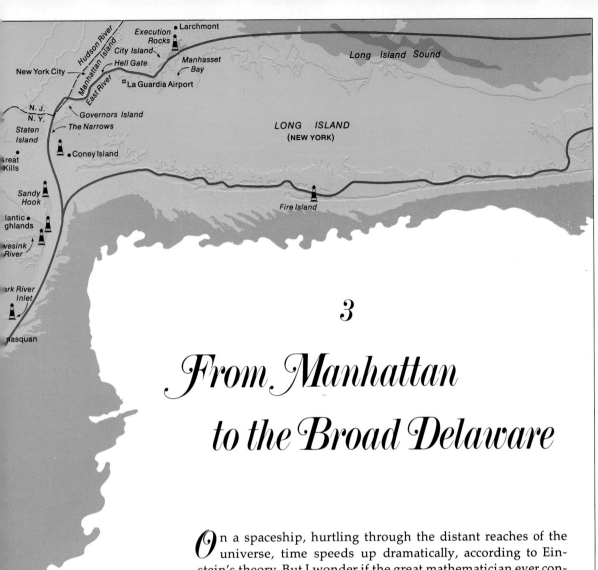

3

From Manhattan
to the Broad Delaware

New Jersey's shallow Waterway winds past resorts and marshes; large boats sail offshore. From Cape May, boatmen navigate Delaware Bay and River to the C & D Canal or on toward Trenton.

*O*n a spaceship, hurtling through the distant reaches of the universe, time speeds up dramatically, according to Einstein's theory. But I wonder if the great mathematician ever considered what happens aboard a slow, happy boat? There, too, time is affected; the hours become as fleeting as cloud shadows, and the days accelerate into a swift progression of weeks.

It seemed like little more than four days, but actually more than four weeks had passed since we had left our starting point at New Bedford. Mike asked a question: "Not counting our side trips, all those zigs and zags off the main route, how far have we come along the Waterway from New Bedford?"

I looked at the Westchester County shore. *Andromeda* sailed not far off Larchmont on a westerly course down the hazy blue reaches of Long Island Sound. We were nearing New York City waters. With considerable effort I juggled a few figures in the part of my mind that had been sketchily imprinted with the rules of arithmetic.

"We've made about 200 miles," I announced.

"That isn't very much," Bill said cheerily. He too did a bit of figuring—but quickly. "We still have about 1,550 miles to go. At this rate it will take us 32 weeks to get to Miami."

We all laughed, unconcerned at our slow pace. We knew it would change in the much more confined southern waters;

73

there *Andromeda* would be motoring and not making as many zigs and zags, as Mike had put it.

Bill took the wheel, and I trained our binoculars on the light and radio beacon, now slowly drawing abeam, that rises in mid-Sound three miles south of Larchmont—an old conical tower on a reef, and close alongside it two drab square buildings and two steel radio towers. The white cone, 62 feet high, wore a red cummerbund about its middle, and was topped by the light in a sort of cupola. The reef on which these structures rested had been built up with riprap, and the entire effect was one of grim, unrelieved harshness.

But perhaps that's the way it should be. We were passing Execution Rocks, traditionally a place of ill omen. Local lore maintains that, prior to the American Revolution, patriots condemned by the king's justices often shouted inflammatory words from the gallows. So the British, goes the story, dug a pit into the rocks and secured iron rings to the walls, and colonials sentenced to death were chained there at low tide and left to drown slowly as the waters rose.

Whatever the origin of the name, it was in use in 1867 when the Federal Government put a lighthouse on the notorious reef. Thereafter, many lightkeepers and their families lived happily at Execution Rocks, and the Coast Guardsmen who now man the station find the site free of ghosts.

Andromeda moved on through waters crowded with every type of pleasure boat, from sailing dinghy to immaculate ocean-going yacht. As we approached City Island, since 1895 a part of New York's sprawling Borough of the Bronx, we picked our way through hundreds of boats that seemed to be milling aimlessly like restive sheep.

City Island surprised us, for it remains a village, quaint and individualistic. Trees line the main thoroughfare, which offers the stroller a *potpourri* of seafood restaurants, shops, stores, honkytonks, and ship chandlers. Short, shady streets with pleasant old homes—the community has 7,000 residents—branch off from the avenue. Boatyards and marinas, all with craft clustered as tightly as aphids, occupy the perimeter of the narrow, mile-long island.

In 1919 Ratsey & Lapthorn, the celebrated sailmakers, built a loft on the water's edge at Schofield Street East. Visitors enter through a small room with a fireplace, plank floors, and dark, paneled walls lined with old photographs of generations of Ratseys and Lapthorns. Upstairs, the floor of the loft's second story, 200 feet long, is covered with huge sheets of red, white, and blue nylon, the colors of Ratsey & Lapthorn's new spinnaker, the Chuting Star. Pieces of sail also strew the floor of the third story, and everywhere workers busy themselves with various tasks, from measuring and cutting to stretching a sail along its luff and finishing the fabric   *(Continued on page 80)*

Silhouetted against the sunrise, New York's Manhattan Bridge links Long Island with Manhattan across the East River. Sailing down the 14-mile-long tidal estuary, Andromeda passed under seven such spans—each a small but impressive part of the engineering miracle that knits the city together.

Churning a frothy wake, the Staten Island ferry crosses the rippled waters
of Upper New York Bay on a summer evening. Battery Park, Manhattan's
verdant front yard, lures strollers to an esplanade along the waterfront
where the Hudson (left) and East Rivers converge. Behind the park
Broadway, once an Indian trail, forms a dark canyon between skyscrapers.
Two round forts—Castle Clinton in Battery Park, and Castle Williams
(far right) on Governors Island—guarded the East River entrance in the
19th century. Twin towers of the World Trade Center, each rising 110
floors above the Hudson, house import and export firms. Uptown, Melissa
Weston (opposite) ends an outing in Central Park with a glass of sangria.

Filleter at Manhattan's Fulton Fish Market, Lou (Champ) Salica pauses in his work to recall winning the world bantamweight title in 1940. Fulton, a wholesale market, opens at 3 a.m. on weekdays, when workers begin unloading 500,000 to a million pounds of seafood and freshwater fish from trucks. At dawn clients inspect the catch and buying begins: Striped bass (below) weigh in on a bucket scale; a fishmonger (bottom) haggles over prices; and a patron (right) carries his halibut home by the tail. By midmorning the market closes, and only scavenger sea gulls and cats remain.

with hand stitching. If the visitor closes his eyes, he can easily imagine himself aboard a sailboat; the nylon as it is rustled about on the floor sounds just like sails luffing in the wind.

G. Colin Ratsey, a tall, almost reedy man of 67, picked up a piece of spinnaker cloth from the floor. "Yes, it's fragile," he said. "This is what we call one-and-a-half-ounce cloth. It's pretty hard to handle if you make it any heavier. You've just got to learn how to use these big, lightweight spinnakers without tearing them."

Like his older brother Ernest, whom we had met at Southport, Connecticut, Mr. Ratsey has rich memories of the America's Cup J-boats, having crewed on the British challenger *Endeavour I*. This pleasant man seems always on the verge of laughter. Perhaps his most joyous memory is of the first Frostbite Regatta, held in 1932 in Manhasset Bay and sailed in dinghies.

"I won that New Year's Day regatta in a snowstorm," he recalled. "It was snowing *and* blowing, and I picked up a crew right off the beach: a man I had never met. I had a bailer, really a little saucepan you'd cook eggs in, and I tied it to a batten and gave it to him. I said, 'Your job is to scrape the snow off the sail.' And that's probably why we won. In those days we had cotton sails, and snow clung to cotton. This nylon would shed the snow."

Then G. Colin Ratsey voiced a philosophy strongly reminiscent of his brother Ernest: "When you've been fooling around with boats all your life, every day is fun. I don't know where my hobby ends and my business begins."

*L*eaving City Island astern, we motored in brilliant sunshine south toward Throgs Neck, a long, skinny peninsula easy to pick up from a distance because of the high bridge linking it with the Borough of Queens. Here we entered the East River — not actually a river but a tidal passage separating Queens and Brooklyn from Manhattan. I gazed up appreciatively at the soaring span as we passed beneath it; no need to worry about *Andromeda*'s 51-foot mast height when going under the engineering marvels that span New York City's waterways. But ahead lay something of real concern, Hell Gate — the narrow, winding channel between Astoria in Queens and Wards Island, a reach of the river swept by powerful tidal currents made erratic and treacherous by an uneven bottom. Through the years Hell Gate has dashed many small boats onto rocks, and prudent yachtsmen attempt the passage only at or near slack tide.

As we neared Rikers Island, planes on their final landing approach to La Guardia Airport passed directly over us, so low that even *Andromeda*'s modest mast seemed about to scrape the underbelly of one of them.

A city prison occupies big, lumpy Rikers Island, and I wondered whether any inmates were watching our progress. It must be difficult enough for men behind bars to see tugboats or freighters freely going about their business; what torment to watch a blithe bird of passage like *Andromeda*.

We passed through the corridor between North and South Brother Islands, and then we entered Hell Gate. My watch said the optimum moment for slack water had occurred 40 minutes earlier. Small whirlpools and striations and burbles marred the surface, but fortunately the tide had not yet begun to race.

Through the years the channel has been considerably improved, but it remains a hazard under poor conditions. A glance at the depth figures on the chart showed the unevenness of the rock-strewn bottom; at one point the depth rose from 116 feet to 35 feet in a distance of about 30 yards. I opened up the throttle briefly, and we went through that strange, tortured bend of the river at better than eight knots.

And now to starboard rose the towers, the monoliths, the glass facades, the soaring concrete and mortar mountains of the Manhattan skyline. Wordless, rapt, each of us lost in a very personal reaction, we watched that incomparable panorama slip slowly past. Manhattan seen from the water is Manhattan without dirt, without the painful struggle for a few feet, a few yards, in the earthworm contractions of its traffic, without its masses of humanity, without the weight upon the spirit of its masonry maze. Gilded by the sun, the great buildings soared up and up with the strength given them by good minds and skeletal steel and straight, clean lines. The supreme urban expression of our age passed in review, and it was deeply moving. San Francisco seen from Marin County and the New York City skyline from the water have always seemed to me the alabaster cities of the American dream, endlessly agleam, with a special hold upon the imaginations of our people.

A quarter of a century earlier, as a young newspaperman, I had worked for five years in Manhattan's pulsing hive and had known it well. Now, without difficulty, I could pick out some of its monumental works—Empire State, RCA, Chrysler—but other buildings, glassily reflecting sun and shadow and cloud, were strangers in a half-remembered land.

Just ahead, Williamsburg Bridge vaulted the river. We passed beneath and made the slow, gradual turn to starboard around Corlears Hook. Two more highways in the sky, the Manhattan and Brooklyn Bridges, crossed our leisurely course; off to starboard that storied thoroughfare, South Street, extended for many blocks along the lower Manhattan waterfront. I reached for the binoculars. Yes, there they were, the half dozen historic old vessels of South Street Seaport Museum, including that still lovely old lady of good breeding, *Wavertree*, a square-rigged merchant ship launched in 1885.

In addition to two piers, the museum owns about 85 percent of all the old buildings in a five-block area. The intent is to restore those dilapidated and forlorn structures to their appearance of a century or more ago when the South Street area was the heart and soul of old New York. Here the great sailing ships, the "sky-rakers," docked in a forest of masts and spars; here they unloaded the myriad products that a booming city devoured, and took aboard the raw materials and manufactures of the maturing republic.

Andromeda continued on past Manhattan's threshold, Battery Park, and the brownstone walls of Castle Clinton, built as a fort in 1811 and later converted into an open-air pavilion called Castle Garden, where Jenny Lind once sang.

Here the Hudson and East Rivers converge, bearing on their tides an amazing and dangerous assortment of flotsam and jetsam. We dodged part of an old piling and kept a wary eye on a ferryboat leaving the Battery for the Statue of Liberty as we passed by Governors Island on our port side.

Both the Dutch and the English used the island as an estate for colonial governors. The Dutch had bought it from the Indians for two ax heads, a string of beads, and a few nails. It later served for many years as a U. S. Army installation; today the Coast Guard uses it as a major headquarters.

Liberty Island lay close off *Andromeda's* starboard beam, and we could see weekend throngs boarding a ferry for the return to Manhattan. More than a million people a year visit the Statue of Liberty, and, as usual, some were looking out of the statue's brow and waving.

*B*ridges of heroic dimension have always seemed to me among the noblest works of man. New York City's newest and most striking bridge, the Verrazano-Narrows, links Brooklyn and Staten Island at The Narrows where Upper Bay joins Lower Bay. A more dramatic site for a bridge could scarcely be imagined. Here man has spun a graceful, slender web of steel and concrete across the entrance to one of the world's great harbors, a kind of triumphal arch above the premier gateway to America. It is the longest suspension bridge on earth.

We sailed beneath its 4,260-foot main span, wondering what that juncture of waters looked like when discovered in 1524 by Giovanni da Verrazano, a Florentine navigator in the service of King Francis I of France. He described it as "a very pleasant place, situated amongst certaine litle steepe hilles . . . there ran down into the sea a great streame. . . ." The river, ironically enough, bears not his name but that of a man who sailed into the harbor 85 years later: Henry Hudson, an Englishman in the employ of the Dutch East India Company.

With some impatience, I watched the shoreline pass by as we hurried toward Great Kills Harbor, a spacious, circular indentation in the southern coast of Staten Island. Thirty-six years earlier I had been a summer visitor at Great Kills. I remembered a sprinkling of shoreside homes, a few docks, some sailboats. We rounded Crookes Point, entered the harbor—and saw boats everywhere! A solid phalanx of marinas stood off to

Rotting hulks disfigure Jersey City's waterfront, directly behind the Statue of Liberty. Some 2,000 abandoned barges, ferryboats, tugs, drydocks, sailing ships, and canal boats clutter areas of New York Harbor. Disintegrating plank by plank, the wrecks produce flotsam that creates a serious navigational hazard.

Stiff breeze billows a spinnaker during a dry run on
City Island, New York. Ratsey & Lapthorn, sailmakers
since 1790, made the racing
sail for a boat named Banjo
Girl. Inside, the third floor
of the firm's loft provides
space for measuring, cutting,
and piecing. Girlie Kettleman
(foreground) and Peggy
Page stitch new sails on
vintage sewing machines.

port, and the hillside above was nearly covered with houses.

A youth of 17 had spent the summer in a house of weathered brown shingles somewhere on that hillside. In the morning and evening the boy sat outside to watch the boats. He had been ill for months, but he was recovering, and he had come to Great Kills for the sea air.

He did a lot of daydreaming; he had never seen sailboats before and they fascinated him: the ease of motion, the quiet, the strange and hurried manipulation of lines when the boats changed course. Someday, he vowed, he would have a sailboat, and he would bring it back to Great Kills.

As we were leaving the next day, I asked Bill to take the wheel so that I could look back upon the armada of boats and the hillside above. Was that the boy's house? Or was it that one? Everything had changed. But no matter. I felt a profound and moving satisfaction. I had kept the promise made by the boy I had been.

New York's large Lower Bay includes Sandy Hook Bay, no small pond itself. Crossing it, we moved into New Jersey waters and overnighted at Atlantic Highlands, where the state has built a big marina protected by a stone sea wall.

Again enjoying fair weather, we picked our way through the buoyage off Sandy Hook, bound for the open Atlantic.

"There are more navigational aids out here than I've ever seen in any one area," Bill remarked. "Look at the chart; it's peppered with them."

"That proves New York has more of everything," said Mike.

But tight-lipped silence soon replaced my wife's normal good humor. *Andromeda* had begun a rhythmic rise and fall with the surge of the open ocean, a motion that Mike's stomach finds objectionable. The wind blew 15 knots or so across our stern, and we ran with the big genoa driving and steadying us and with an assist from the engine, since we had gotten a late start. In times of stress my wife knits. The Intracoastal Waterway proved a two-sweater voyage.

All boats running down the New Jersey coast must take to the open sea from Sandy Hook to Manasquan. From there, shallow-draft boats without tall masts can run inside on the New Jersey Intracoastal Waterway all the way to Cape May. But that route, area boatmen warned me, had shoaled to three feet and less in numerous places and could not be traversed by a vessel of *Andromeda*'s size. So, like many other boating gypsies, we planned to sail down the New Jersey coast in three easy hops: Manasquan, Atlantic City, Cape May, each with inlets from the sea safe to run in good weather.

We stayed a respectful distance off low-lying Sandy Hook but still enjoyed a good look at its light, dating from 1762 — the oldest continuously operating lighthouse in the Western Hemisphere. Sandy Point boasts a state park, and so does Beacon Hill, farther south along the coast. There, high above the ocean, we could see the distinctive Navesink Twin Lights. Both towers once flashed brilliant beacons. Today only the north tower is operative — from May 15 to October 15.

Andromeda ran into Manasquan Inlet through two parallel breakwaters extending out to sea, and on Sunday afternoon this rather narrow slot contained boats of every size and description, some racing in, some out, beating the water into a white maelstrom. In the midst of this chaos several small boats lay at anchor, their owners — unbelievably — attempting to fish, despite battering wakes and the imminent danger of being sliced in half. As if threading our way through a mine field, we motored into the relative safety of the crowded harbor and squeezed our way into a narrow berth at a marina near a bascule railroad bridge at the entrance to the New Jersey waterway.

Carefully applying the fourth undercoat to a Post 40 Sportfisherman, Albert Rundio earns his title of "Picasso" at Post Marine Company in Mays Landing, New Jersey. Still using wood construction, Post's work force of 50 people skillfully handcraft 25 to 30 boats each year. Builders (opposite) plank a hull with Western red cedar, a lightweight wood of excellent durability.

Here we had a ringside seat at the Battle of Manasquan River. Boats in seemingly endless numbers passed beneath the bridge; because of the bridge's supports, those coming from the inlet could not see those emerging from the waterway, and vice versa. Collisions seemed inevitable, yet somehow were always avoided. To complicate matters, the tide had begun racing out toward the inlet, as if the churned water longed for the quiet of the dark ocean depths.

The sight of so many yachtsmen pursuing pleasure so assiduously in the midst of utter bedlam struck us as funny, and we began laughing uncontrollably.

Taking from my pocket a pad and pencil, I began a count of the passing boats. In 20 minutes I totaled 103. A young New Jersey marine policeman, patrolling in a small boat, called to me: "If you're counting boats, you'd better get more paper! But actually, this is mild. The Coast Guard says 6,000 boats have passed through the bridge between 6 and 4:30 on a holiday."

Moments later a bell clanged, and the bridge lowered. Pandemonium! Scores of boats threw their engines in reverse, then dodged and turned as those behind bore down on them. Soon

Oasis of luxuriant cordgrass attracts common egrets in Brigantine National Wildlife Refuge, more than 19,000 acres of salt marsh, tidal bays, and channels north of Atlantic City. Once considered wasteland, New Jersey salt marshes were dredged and filled for "lagoon developments." Small houses on narrow strips of landfill replaced the hardy cordgrass that nurtures marsh wildlife. At last recognizing the importance of its coastal wetlands, the state passed legislation in 1970 to prevent further destruction of this vital area.

the traffic backed up all the way to the inlet. Taking advantage of the melee, the smallest boats tried to work their way nearer the bridge, hoping to be first in line when it reopened. Horns blew, helmsmen shouted, crewmen fended off other vessels with boathooks.

When the bridge reopened, a second policeman in a small boat tried to maintain some sort of order, calling out, "Slow down! Stay in line! Keep your distance!" We watched from our snug berth, glad to be spectators and not competitors.

Next morning we clawed our way offshore, seeking sea room in choppy waters. The low shoreline en route to Atlantic City is essentially featureless; so we were all happy when Bill's sharp eyes picked up an unmistakable landmark, old Barnegat Light. It's no longer in service, but in daytime it still pinpoints some nasty shoals extending well to sea.

Atlantic City's inlet, protected by two parallel breakwaters, looks much like Manasquan's but is deeper and wider. Here, too, speeding powerboats beat the water with the relentlessness of an electric mixer whipping meringue, but we made our way unscathed to the big state-owned marina.

All of Andromeda's crew had been to Atlantic City at one time or another, and we found that famous resort not greatly changed. Some old landmarks such as the Traymore Hotel had vanished, but there stood a hostelry I remembered favorably, Chalfonte-Haddon Hall. We had a splendid dinner of steak Diane in one of its dining rooms, and afterward, on the crowded boardwalk, enjoyed the same things we had years ago: buying saltwater taffy, shooting at targets, having our sketches made by sidewalk artists.

In bland, hazy weather, we cruised under power to Cape May. Its inlet, shielded by the now-familiar stone breakwaters, and its inner harbor formed a big, roomy L. We tied up at a marina with floating docks, an amenity that made it much easier for us to get on and off Andromeda.

At each stop, gregarious Bill Gay looked over all the boats and met many young people. But he hadn't been on shore leave in Cape May more than 15 minutes when he reappeared.

"There's another Gulfstar motorsailer here, a 36-footer, with a family going down the Intracoastal," he told me. "The boat's name is Nevermore, with a dinghy called Quoth."

On the dock that evening I met the boat's owner, tall, mustachioed Gene Hebert, a man in his mid-30's who had recently quit his job as a newscaster with a television and radio network in New York City. Gene and his wife, Carol, had sold their suburban home and now lived aboard Nevermore with their three small children.

"Nevermore the New York rat race! That's the story behind the boat's name," Gene said with feeling. "I've had it with that life. The name never lets me forget New York is over and done with; and little *Quoth* reminds me of how often I've said, 'never-more!' We're on our way to St. Thomas in the Virgin Islands, where we're going to live. But there's no hurry. I'm doing spot work for the network on the way south, and I think we'll stop in Miami long enough to put Deirdre, the oldest child, in school for a semester."

Gene and I didn't know it then, but our paths would cross often all the way to central Florida, and *Andromeda*'s crew would develop a great respect for *Nevermore*'s self-sufficient, happy little family, pioneers 20th-century style.

Cape May is a very pleasant town containing a treasure trove of Victorian architecture, and it may have been America's first resort. An advertisement in 1766 in the *Pennsylvania Gazette* described its beach as a place "where a number resort for Health and Bathing in the Water." Later the community became known as the "summer home of Presidents." Today Cape May residents preserve the Victorian atmosphere with many faithful restorations of old homes and stores.

On the morning of our departure for the Chesapeake, thick fog enveloped the harbor. I wanted no part of sailing in that soup. Moreover, that day we had a special problem. A bridge only 55 feet above the water spans Cape May Canal leading into Delaware Bay; I did not care to squeeze under it on an abnormally high tide with a 51-foot mast topped by a three-foot radio antenna. That meant we would have to go out the inlet into the ocean and sail around the cape into Delaware Bay. That would present no problem in good weather—but in fog?

Impatiently we waited until the fog lifted enough for us to start out the inlet for a look. But only halfway out the mist seemed as palpable as a wall, and I turned back for the harbor.

Andromeda had just completed the turn when, from the direction of Cape May, a big yawl emerged from the gray and passed close to port. I recognized her almost immediately: *White Mist,* a blue-water beauty whose cruises have been featured in many a NATIONAL GEOGRAPHIC article. At the helm was her owner, Melville Bell Grosvenor, the National Geographic Society's chairman and editor-in-chief.

As *White Mist* swept by, I asked myself: Could I slink back into Cape May after the fog-be-damned example of my boss? Mike and Bill agreed we should turn about again, and we set out in pursuit.

Soon we could make out the yawl's masts and spars, then her graceful white hull. We pulled abeam but well off to starboard. It was my intent to stick closely to the shore of the cape, which Bill Gay could see intermittently, and grope our way slowly under power around to the entrance of the Cape May Canal. The water was deep close to the land; our course would keep us inshore of shoals; and when we got to the canal we could decide whether or not to chance a run up the bay on a course that would keep us well away from big ships.

Mel Grosvenor, however, set sail to catch the slight breeze, and vanished into the fog toward the shipping lanes.

For the next hour and a half, we worked our way around the Cape. Occasionally something darker than the mist would loom to starboard; that would be the land, or, frequently, a stone jetty. Bells rang aboard anchored boats we seldom saw, and once we got a glimpse of a man ringing a bell on the end of a jetty, apparently to warn vessels off the rocks. A fishing boat loomed dead ahead, but it slipped by on the reciprocal of our course, probably following the shore as we were. Bill stood in *Andromeda*'s bow, motioning me to steer port or starboard, and Mike kept watch from astern. Finally we found the canal entrance, and anchored among other boats waiting for the veil to lift.

*E*ventually it did, partially, and a little past noon I decided that if we left immediately we could just make the Chesapeake and Delaware Canal before dark. Off we went Across-the-Flats, as yachtsmen call the shallow water route to the east of Delaware Bay's shipping lanes.

Twenty minutes after our fresh start the fog closed in again. But, having committed ourselves, we pushed on, seeing nothing, hearing nothing. Nearly three hours later we chanced upon a big bell buoy; it marked the ship channel and told me immediately we were far off course. I had made too little allowance for the ebb tide, and its strong currents had set us nearly two nautical miles west of where I thought we were.

But nature, having chastened us, decided to treat us with favor. The fog melted away, the sun came out brilliantly, the tide changed, and a good breeze and following sea helped us up the bay. Just at dusk we reached the Delaware side of the C & D Canal and motored through its well-lighted reaches. Near the Chesapeake entrance the Corps of Engineers has built a comfortable little anchorage. We slipped in, found it empty, and dropped the hook for a quiet and restful night.

I awakened early the next morning and clambered up into the cockpit. Some fog had crept in, but I knew from the golden quality of the early light that it would soon burn off. Then, across the anchorage, I noticed *White Mist,* as motionless in the still water as a boat upon canvas. Unheard by us, she had ghosted in during the hours of darkness.

On the yawl, too, a crewman appeared, and soon there was other activity topside. Both boats left the anchorage at about the same time, and we had an opportunity to identify ourselves. The two crews talked back and forth for a while; Mel reported a close shave in darkness and fog with a mountainous freighter transiting the canal.

Then both boats moved out into the Chesapeake toward Annapolis, eager for home. Through a lovely blue and gold morning, *White Mist* sailed for Gibson Island, *Andromeda* for that serene and special place, Church Creek.

Barnegat Inlet allows cautious passage from the Atlantic into protected New Jersey waters. To the north across the inlet, pristine sand dunes border Barnegat Bay (top); villages of Long Beach Island stretch south from red-and-white Barnegat Light. For 70 years, "Old Barney" flashed warnings of treacherous shoals. Near the beacon's tower, the bay lures Sunday sailors and fishermen.

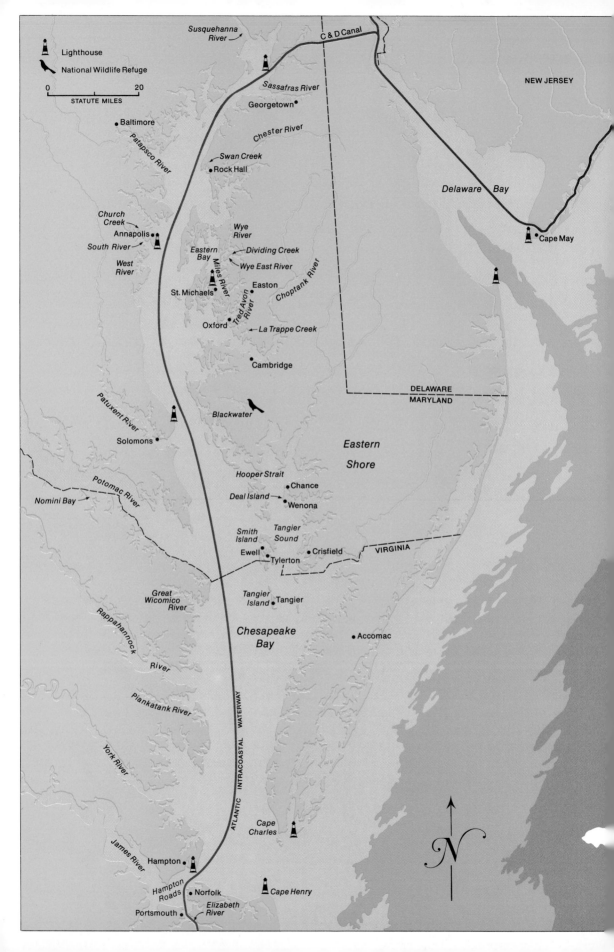

4

The Water World of the Chesapeake

*T*he Bay. If you live on its shores, or if a gracious and kindly Providence once permitted you to live there, "the Bay" can only mean the Chesapeake, an eighth sea in the thinking of many of its residents, a place the Creator must have fashioned while practicing for the larger handiwork of Paradise.

A parochial view, to be sure — but not without point. Consider, first, the Chesapeake's sheer size. It extends nearly 200 miles, with a width varying from 4 to 30 miles. Some 150 rivers, creeks, and branches empty into it, forming by far the largest estuarial system on the Atlantic Coast. Its tidewater shoreline totals more than 7,000 miles. One could spend most of a lifetime exploring the coves and crannies of this maze by boat and never go back to the same place twice.

Moreover, despite the impact of a growing population and the advent of new heavy industry, the Chesapeake remains a place of extraordinary beauty. Only a small part of its shoreline has yet been touched by commercial development and industrial blight. The Eastern Shore, in particular, looks from the water much as it always has. Here you will seek in vain for the wave-battered rocks and crags of a Maine, an Oregon, or a California. The Chesapeake's beauty is quiet, gentle, sylvan: the broad, placid river flowing past estates with histories much older than that of the nation; the stream that meanders with delightful indecision through woodland and field; the wide estuary, its low-lying shores broken by creeks that lure as compellingly as any siren song.

Many Chesapeake people will testify that the Bay imparts to

Almost 200 miles long, Chesapeake Bay offers endless variety along Maryland and Virginia shorelines cut by scores of rivers, creeks, and coves rich in history and watermen's tradition.

their lives a special quality, something more than just the opportunity for relaxation and water fun. It might be called an appreciation of fundamental values: the beauty of nature and concern for its fragility, the importance of solitude, a realization that change is not synonymous with progress, an awareness of the rich heritage from an earlier America—all these things are part of it, part of something that varies with the individual and yet is nonetheless real. It stems, I am sure, from proximity to those vast and timeless waters, to things as basic as tides and storms, the migration of waterfowl and the catching of fish, the set of a sail and the plunge of an osprey.

Captain John Smith succumbed to the Chesapeake's spell during two voyages of exploration in 1608. He prepared one of the earliest maps of the Bay, and on it one can recognize such rivers as the James, Rappahannock, Potomac, Patuxent, Patapsco, Susquehanna, and Sassafras. With the map, he published in 1612 a "Description," which had this to say of the waters he had entered through Capes Charles and Henry:

"Within is a country that may haue the prerogatiue over the most pleasant places of Europe, Asia, Africa, or America, for large and pleasant navigable rivers: heaven and earth never agreed better to frame a place for mans habitation....

Here are mountaines, hils, plaines, valeyes, rivers and brookes all running most pleasantly into a faire Bay compassed but for the mouth with fruitfull and delightsome land."

No gathering of boatmen could possibly agree on what season is best on this distinctive part of the Intracoastal Waterway. In spring, eager to shed the scales of winter, we sail forth into a world reborn, with dogwood snowy on the shores and stiff breezes to carry us afar. Summer is somnolent and lazy, a time to seek out the headwaters leisurely and dream away the soft nights. But autumn—that can be very special. The shores blaze, the winds gust, and down from the north come the beloved invaders. More than a million waterfowl descend upon the Chesapeake during the autumn migration.

The Bay provided the most idyllic day I can recall on the water. It occurred late one October on a cruise from Georgetown, near the head of the Sassafras River, to Swan Creek, tucked away in the serrated land just north of the Chester River's mouth. At that time Mike and I owned an earlier *Andromeda*, a 35-foot ketch stoutly built of oak and mahogany. We had aboard two friends from Mobile, Alabama, Bill Sturgeon and his wife,

Fleet of gleaming new pleasure craft occupies the Annapolis city dock during the annual U. S. Sailboat Show. The exhibit includes boats of all sizes, from small dinghies to ocean-going yachts. Inside the striped tents, booths display marine navigational and communications equipment and other boating accessories. Above, a prospective customer studies a sales brochure.

Spinnakers filled by an October breeze, cruising-class sailboats compete in the Annapolis Yacht Club's Fall Series on the Chesapeake. Boat owners traveling south on the Intracoastal Waterway sometimes interrupt the journey to enter Chesapeake races. Near the starting line of the course, southeast of Annapolis, stands Thomas Point Shoal Light (above), originally constructed in 1825 and rebuilt 50 years later. Two Coast Guardsmen operate the station, the Bay's last manned lighthouse off shore, but plans call for its conversion to automatic controls by 1976.

Mary Sands, and I hoped my Bay would show her best face.

She did. The sun shone from a cloudless blue that had the scoured look October brings, and the high, wooded shores of the Sassafras were a gantlet of flame for us to run.

At the mouth of the river the breeze freshened, and we began a glorious romp down the Bay on a close reach, a sail to remember in the doldrums of summer and by the hearth in winter. Main, genoa, mizzen took on the taut contours of sails driving hard in a fair and prodigal wind. Bill trimmed the sheets, I took my hands from the wheel, and *Andromeda*, in perfect balance with wind and wave, steered herself straight and true.

To avoid crossing shallow Swan Point Bar, we sailed well south of our destination, then turned north and worked our way past Rock Hall and into the sheltered anchorage of Swan Creek. The sun had dropped low in the sky, and echelon after echelon of honking Canada geese flew overhead, quitting the grainfields where they had been feeding to seek the shelter of the Chester and its tributaries. Soon the sun died flamboyantly, and still the geese passed overhead, and flocks of swift, low-flying ducks. An immense harvest moon rose, and a skein of geese crossed its face, black silhouettes on an orange paper cutout.

Despite the chill, we lingered long in the cockpit, unwilling to admit a day so perfect could end. In a sense it didn't end, and it won't—not as long as one of us remembers.

*A*nyone who cruises the Chesapeake has his favorite anchorages. I am particularly fond of Dividing Creek off the Wye East River on Maryland's Eastern Shore. Except for the entrance, tall trees surround it, giving a sense of walled-off solitude to the narrow waters. Winds seldom ruffle that dark surface where, as on polished slate, the overhanging trees cast their images, heightening the feeling of enclosure. Distantly, through the mouth of the creek and across the Wye East, one can see a farmhouse, the only sign of habitation.

Into Dividing Creek we eased one summer evening at dusk. The familiar waters lay invitingly empty, and Mike and I and our daughters settled down for a thoroughly selfish enjoyment of our favorite creek. Stars soon filled the narrow breach overhead, shining with a crystalline hardness and clarity rare in summer. We watched them slowly set beneath the trees while other bright worlds took their places, and we listened to the cacophony of insects and the repetitive, cadenced notes of a whippoorwill. Finally my crew sought their bunks, leaving the night to me.

Perhaps I drowsed, for suddenly I found myself standing in the cockpit, peering into the darkness and not knowing why. Then came again the cry that must have awakened me, a prolonged *hooooo-hoooo-hooo*. An owl, quite loud and nearby. To my surprise I heard a second, third, and fourth cry, all in rather quick succession and all from different directions. While other

Flinging capfuls of water, exuberant plebes drench one another in a fountain while celebrating the completion of their first year at the United States Naval Academy in Annapolis. June Week, six days of ceremonies and festivities, signals the end of the academic year and, for fourth-year men, their graduation and commissioning. At right, midshipmen shoulder rifles and move onto Worden Field for a dress parade.

nocturnal creatures hushed, as if listening too, the calls continued, some distant, some near, until the moonless night belonged solely to the owls.

Could there be only two? Could they be flying about so they seemed everywhere amid those leafy walls? I strained my eyes, hoping to see a shadow against the stars. But I glimpsed nothing, and that chorus, the strangest I ever heard, continued from all about me for perhaps 20 minutes.

The next morning my family said, "What owls?" They had slept soundly. But for me it had been a magic night. I felt I had overheard some strange avian communion that humans were not supposed to share.

*I*f I have made the Chesapeake sound a bit like Eden, it's because it is. But can it remain that way? Strong pressures of population growth and industrialization exist, yet the situation has its positive and hopeful aspects.

The Bay is continually studied, sampled, examined, and probed by a consortium of scientists from the University of Maryland, Johns Hopkins University, the Smithsonian Institution, and the Virginia Institute of Marine Science. Their efforts, along with those of the Corps of Engineers and other groups, assure sound information on which to base future decisions.

Until now industrial development has been limited very largely to the western side, principally in the areas of Baltimore in the northern part of the Bay and Norfolk in the southern.

Despite pollution of some tributaries, the Chesapeake so far remains healthy. Tides and currents flush and renew it, sustaining a very complex life system. Estuaries contain some creatures that exist mostly in salt water, others that live in fresh water, and still others that need a mix of both. Many fish spawn in the rivers and streams, and the Bay long has been famous for its oysters and crabs.

On Church Creek we have our own ecological problem: recurrent siltation in the headwaters from a storm drain and nearby construction. But this lovely tidal stream is as yet unspoiled. It cuts into Annapolis Neck from the South River for about a mile and a half. Almost all the left bank remains undeveloped and densely wooded; on the right bank an occasional house, carefully sited, stands among the trees. Just upstream from our place, nature has sculptured a snug cove. Occasionally we anchor there in *Andromeda,* even though it's little more than a stone's throw from our dock. In spring and fall boats traveling the Intracoastal Waterway rest in the cove. We read the distant hailing ports on their transoms and wave as they pass our house.

Church Creek and neighboring Crab Creek enfold between them a peninsula, part of larger Annapolis Neck, that remains rural even though at its mainland end it adjoins the Annapolis city line. It contains planted fields and horse pastures, hedgerows and woodlands. Swans and ducks winter on the two creeks.

Residents feed them, and the ducks seem to trust us even while other ducks are being shot on the South River. We permit no hunting on the creeks or peninsula, and quail, doves, squirrels, rabbits, raccoons, muskrats, and possums are commonplace. I have seen deer, and—only once—a fox.

The historic old city of Annapolis holds much of the Chesapeake's special ambience, and we count ourselves lucky to live on its doorstep. The Continental Congress met in Maryland's handsome brick State House at Annapolis; there George Washington resigned as Commander-in-Chief of the Continental Army; and there the United States ratified the Treaty of Paris, ending the Revolutionary War.

Part of the city has been designated a national historic district. My wife and I never tire of wandering about its narrow streets, many with houses so old and so tiny that they seem to huddle together for mutual protection against the 20th century. Most streets run down to the harbor, where oystermen sell their catches and fishermen and clammers tie up among the yachts. On Wednesday nights in summer we watch sailboat races from the Annapolis Yacht Club or from the sea wall of the Naval Academy. Each October, at the city dock, we attend those crowded, colorful spectacles, the U. S. Sailboat Show and the U. S. Powerboat Show.

But best of all is a stroll about Annapolis on May Day. Then homes and stores alike hang baskets of flowers at their front doors. Each year our ritual inspection includes making sure that the Naval Academy has placed a big basket on the guardhouse at Gate One, and that the little shelter for the bridge tender on the Spa Creek drawbridge has its diminutive May basket.

Some of the finest old homes in Maryland lie in the countryside southwest of Annapolis. George Washington dined at the magnificent Georgian mansion, Tulip Hill, on his way to and from the races at Annapolis in 1771, and he must have ridden his horse beneath the tulip poplars, some still standing, that gave the estate its name. Scores of times I have used those huge trees as landmarks when sailing into the West River.

*C*hesapeake watermen comprise a group as old, proud, and clannish as any of the landed gentry. For centuries members of the same families have pursued oystering, crabbing, and fishing in the Chesapeake's fecund waters.

But that way of life is changing. Not many young men want to wrest a living from the water, particularly on the oyster boats. Under a Maryland conservation law, oyster dredging must be done by sailboats. Until recently the boats were not permitted to dredge under power, and even now they can do so only two days a week. These are the hardy old skipjacks, jib-and-mainsail-rigged, with raked masts and clipper bows. Their crews take them out from late to early spring, "drudgin'," as they pronounce it, for "arsters" on bars they call "rocks."

Capt. Dewey Webster, 75, of Deal Island owned and sailed the *Mary W. Sommers* for years—"prettiest skipjack ever built," he says—and before her the *Richard Lee*—"fastest on Tangier Sound." He has witnessed the long decline of oystering.

"I remember as a boy I could count a hundred boats all workin' at once on just one drudge rock in the sound, Turtle Egg," said Captain Webster. "Now there's only about 30 skipjacks left on all the Chesapeake. The crews got right smart age on 'em, too. There's not many drudge boat captains under 50.

"You can work skipjacks in winds up to 25 miles an hour—all depends on where you are and how big the seas get. So it blows right pert drudgin' those rocks, and it rains and it snows. But it's not the exposure that's so bad. With plenty to do you can keep warm; but man, it's turrible hard work."

Other working sailboats, the lumber schooners, plied the Chesapeake until not long before World War II. My friend Capt. Irwin (Roy) Jenkins sailed on one of the most famous of the old schooners, *Mattie F. Dean,* when he was 14. Today at 56 Roy is a licensed master of ocean-going yachts and chief pilot of the Atlantic Coast Pilots, an organization that delivers large pleasure craft up and down the seaboard. But he was born into a waterman's family on the lower Potomac River.

"*Mattie Dean*'s captain said he'd give me a dollar a month for each year of my age—so I got $14," Roy recalls. "We had cordwood stacked on deck, and I had to saw and split it to fit the stove's firebox. I cooked for five men, made bread, and washed dishes. That was while I was resting—because I helped hoist the sails, heave the anchor, and load and unload cargo.

"I remember sailing that schooner from Nomini Bay, Virginia —30 miles up the Potomac—to Baltimore between sunup and sundown. That's a good 125 miles. We went up the Bay in an 18- to 20-knot sou'wester, sailing wing and wing, the mainsail boomed out on one side, the foresail on the other, and the jib drawing in the middle. Even had the topsail on her. And we drove her so hard those loaded decks were awash."

Not one of the old schooners still sails. Their remnants rot in tidal marshes, and each year tired old skipjacks join them. Yet many of the little hidden ports of call that these boats served, and the creeks and backwaters leading to them, remain virtually unchanged. When the world and its works weigh upon me, I vanish into the maze of the Chesapeake, where the past is never far away, ready to be entered like a sanctuary.

*T*he past still pleasantly flavors, though it no longer envelops, the two most popular yachting centers on the Eastern Shore. Quiet bywaters can be balm, but for convivial fun, for raft-ups with friends on other boats, we often sail to St. Michaels or Oxford, both in Talbot County, Maryland.

While we were working together on this book, Jim Amos decided we needed a break and suggested an overnight cruise from

ROBERT W. MADDEN (BELOW AND RIGHT)

Hard-shell blue crabs provide a feast for Bill Gay, Allan and Mike Fisher, and neighbor Stacy Lyttle at a restaurant in St. Michaels, Maryland. A live crab puzzles a Chesapeake Bay retriever. On Smith Island, holding floats yield newly molted soft-shell crabs.

ROBERT W. MADDEN (ABOVE)

Graceful dowager of the Chesapeake, the skipjack **Ruby G. Ford** (above), built in 1891, runs before blustery winds on a winter's day of oyster dredging. Now rapidly disappearing, skipjacks once formed part of a large fleet of working sailboats that plied the Bay during the first quarter of the 20th century. Above left, skipjack captain Clifton Webster joins members of his crew for lunch in the cabin of the **Maggie Lee**. On the boat's deck, a crewman culls oysters while the dredge, operated by a power winch, scrapes the shellfish off the Bay bottom and hauls them up in a net (left).

Church Creek to St. Michaels. So, with Mike aboard, we freed *Andromeda* from her lines and motored out into the South River to sniff the air. A southwest breeze—good. Up went the main, the jenny unfurled with a few good pulls on the sheet, and off we went at seven knots on a reach. But, as often happens, our nice little wind proved to be a land breeze and it died at the river's mouth. Crossing the Bay, we got a southeast wind bang on the nose and took aboard occasional showers of spray. As helmsman, I caught them right in the face.

Eastern Bay put us on a northeasterly heading, and the breeze, though it sagged at times, kept *Andromeda* moving along at four to five knots. We enjoyed a very indolent and undemanding jog until the wind died as we turned into the Miles River.

No one could miss the turn from the Miles into St. Michaels harbor. Off to starboard we could see two exhibits of the Chesapeake Bay Maritime Museum: the old Hooper Strait lighthouse, a hexagonal wooden structure on pilings, gleaming with fresh white paint, and a tubby old lightship, red as a barn. We slipped past them to a waterfront restaurant.

If Chesapeake gourmets had to single out the area's supreme delicacy, it might well be steamed crabs. At the restaurant a waitress stacked two dozen huge crabs on a table alongside *Andromeda,* and we joyously cracked and ate them with the appetites of longshoremen.

Oxford bears small resemblance to St. Michaels. The town has not one harbor but two, and the outer lies on a broad stretch of the calm Tred Avon River. Near the municipal dock rises the Robert Morris Inn, named for the merchant who once lived here; he was the father of Robert Morris, the Revolutionary War patriot and financier. A long main street lined with handsome frame houses, meticulously kept, extends back from the outer harbor. Most of Oxford's waterfront, however, adjoins sheltered Town Creek, location of some of the finest marinas to be found anywhere along the Intracoastal Waterway.

Oxford's municipal fireworks display on the Fourth of July is a rousing show staged at the Tred Avon Yacht Club in the outer harbor. Boatmen have the best seats because all the aerial displays burst over the water. Boats start to assemble off the yacht club at noon, and by dusk hundreds lie at anchor in the river, some rafted together six and seven deep.

*W*e had been home from northern waters only a few weeks when the first tinges of red and gold along Church Creek told us it was time to head south. As crew, in addition to Mike and Bill Gay, we signed aboard Mrs. Virginia Finnegan, an editorial assistant at the National Geographic Society and my close colleague for 21 years. Despite a drizzle and a light southerly that made us resort to the diesel, we felt happy and expectant. The fall migration of boats had begun, and we hoped to meet some interesting fellow migrants.

Composite print of six photographs taken from a satellite 562 miles above Chesapeake Bay combines monochrome and infrared exposures. Such montages help scientists study plant cover, geology, and water resources. Red indicates vegetation; light blue traces river sedimentation after a rainstorm. Clouds show as white flecks, offshore islands and shoals as long, thin white strips.

EARTH RESOURCES TECHNOLOGY SATELLITE-1, NASA

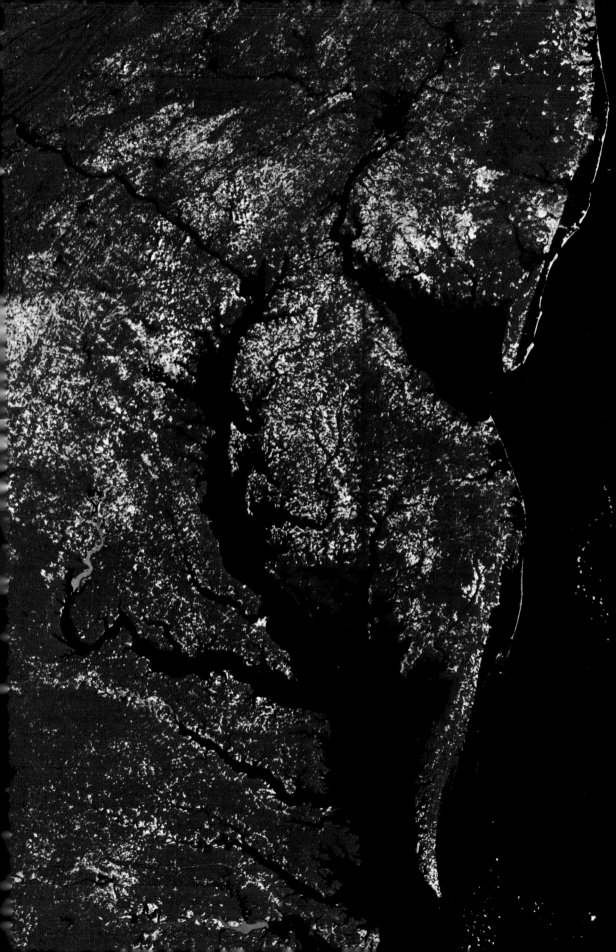

Boats lie anchored in the peaceful waters of La Trappe Creek, Maryland, off the Choptank River (top). In t

reground stands Boston, a colonial house gutted by fire in the mid-19th century but restored in recent years.

Solomons, a homely little hodgepodge near the mouth of the Patuxent, remains basically a fisherman's town with a strong admixture now of rollicking yachtsmen. We skirted the shoal known locally as Molly's Leg and took a slip at Zahniser's Marina. Next to *Andromeda* lay an old wooden cutter, *Fibalot*, with a long bowsprit. Her owner, a retired Air Force colonel named Jim Shumard, and his two sons, Jimi and Davi, were scrubbing her down. "For years I've wanted to do this Water-

way," he said. "I bought *Fibalot* in 1968 after returning from Southeast Asia, and I got her with retirement and this trip in mind. So now we're leaving the Washington area, bound for Orlando, Florida."

The colonel, youthful-looking and trim with dark hair, said he had enjoyed sailing for years. Why sailing, I asked, instead of golf? Or tennis? He thought a moment. "You can correlate it to flying, the freedom you have when you pilot a plane," he said. "To being your own master—and in combat with the elements." A big, happy smile suc-

Morning mist veils a ketch in La Trappe Creek on the Chesapeake's Eastern Shore. A favorite overnight spot for boats cruising the Bay, the creek offers quiet shelter and a white sand beach for swimmers. Visiting boatmen can obtain supplies at the nearby town of Cambridge, and glimpse colonial Maryland in the old farmsteads along La Trappe's banks.

ceeded this bit of philosophy. "From now on, *Fibalot* and I are going to see a lot of each other," said the colonel.

Minutes later, on the pier, I stopped to admire a beard more resplendent than my own and found myself shaking hands with yet another Waterway gypsy, Lionel Willens, a retired jeweler from Detroit. Robust and powerfully built, he didn't resemble my concept of a jeweler. But Lionel said he had whipped himself into shape during the long cruise from Detroit aboard his 35-foot sloop *Lanikai* (Hawaiian for "heavenly waters"). With his wife, Gert, and daughter, Kathy, he had sailed Lake St. Clair, the Detroit River, Lake Erie, the Erie Canal, and the Hudson, then down the New Jersey coast and up the Delaware.

"We're on our way to Sarasota, Florida, where we've bought a condominium," Lionel said. "But we're taking our time."

I told him we would leave in the morning for Deal, Smith, and Tangier Islands, among the last strongholds of the Chesapeake watermen and the old way of life. The latter two islands, I said, lay far offshore, and their villages were probably the most remote and isolated places on the Bay. Lionel thought he might follow us, and the next day he did.

Headed again by a light southeaster, we motored across the Bay, through Hooper Strait, and down Tangier Sound to Deal. Though I had never called there before, it seemed familiar. Islands in the southern Chesapeake look much alike: sandy, low-lying, and featureless, fringed by tidal marshes, with clusters of frame and shingle houses usually perched on pilings.

By the time we attained a slip in the little buttonhook harbor at Chance, on the Eastern Shore mainland only a few hundred yards from Deal Island, the wind had picked up to a gusty 15 to 20 knots. But later the wind died, Bill launched the dinghy, and he and Virginia rowed across the harbor to a seafood packing plant, returning with big buckets of oysters. The Willenses joined us in the assault on the oysters, and soon we added to our group three brothers, Bob, Frank, and Nelson Daniel. Bob, from Royal Oak, Maryland, owned a 35-foot sloop, and he said that once each year he and his brothers cruised together either on the Chesapeake or on Long Island Sound.

*T*he next day Cpl. Robert Kraft of the Maryland Marine Police took me around and about the island in his Boston Whaler. The Deal Island area still can claim nearly half of the skipjacks on the Chesapeake, most of them at Wenona, a tiny place at the island's southern end. But not all were there; I counted only six. Scaling, streaked, battered, sails old and worn—they seemed a dejected lot. But nothing could spoil the graceful lines of bow and sheer, and each would soon get her annual fall overhaul.

We found *Bernice J*, a skipjack built in 1904 at Accomac, Virginia, cradled in a lift while owner Charles Abbott and first mate Jim Cannon gravely inspected her bottom. I could have tossed silver dollars through a couple of gaps in her planks, and the wood felt "sobby"—the watermen's wonderful term for waterlogged. "I won't let her die," said Abbott. "We'll fix her up. She's been a good girl in her day."

On an overcast morning, but with a favoring breeze from the northeast, we sailed for Smith Island. Ewell, one of three communities on the island, qualifies for the adjective "quaint" more than any other spot on the Chesapeake. It can claim two main streets, one a waterway lined with rickety, spindly piers and sagging, weatherbeaten crab cribs, the other a narrow roadway flanked by neat little homes with minuscule front yards. Smith has no municipal building, no jail—indeed, no government. Practically everyone belongs to the United Methodist Church, and the church officials provide the leadership. A few old cars, brought over by boat, run up and down the one road. Until recently the cars were unlicensed. I recalled one substantial dock, owned by the county, so we tied up there.

Three mail, freight, and passenger boats, *Island Star, Island Belle,* and *Miss Whitelock,* link the island with Crisfield on the Eastern Shore. When the *Star* whistled her afternoon arrival, I walked down to the pier to talk *(Continued on page 118)*

Autumn sun rises over flocks of Canada geese arriving at Blackwater National Wildlife Refuge, about ten miles south of Cambridge, Maryland. Thousands of the geese winter in the vicinity of Chesapeake Bay. Elsewhere on the Eastern Shore, fall brings out the hunters (below). Brothers Lem and Steve Ward (opposite) look over some of the decoys they carve and paint in their workshop at Crisfield. "Counterfeits from nature," the Wards call the wooden waterfowl they have been making since 1918. Coveted as objects of art, the most detailed of their decoys bring high prices; the Canada goose in the foreground, for example, sold for $1,000.

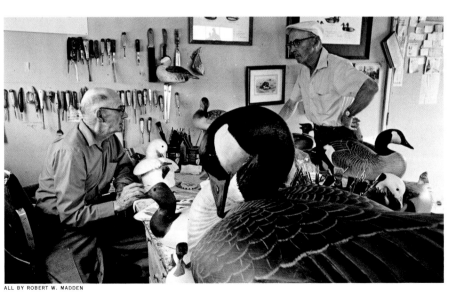

ALL BY ROBERT W. MADDEN

115

Clustered on narrow springboards over the water, the crew of a log canoe balances the fast but unstable craft during a race from St. Michaels to the Wye East River. Hewn from logs first fastened together with wooden pegs, the high-masted, top-heavy canoes—unique to the Chesapeake—once served as workboats for oystering and crabbing. After the race, competitors assemble for a party at the riverside estate of the Peter Hersloffs. Lettering on one guest's shorts identifies her as a crew member of the canoe Mystery. Another participant quenches his thirst.

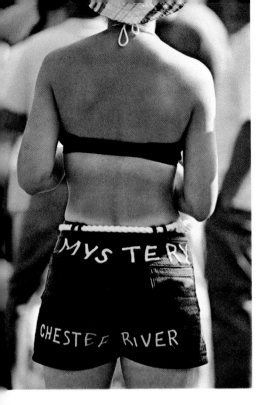

with Frank Dize, the owner and operator. With practiced ease, he brought *Star* in while carrying on several conversations.

"Did you get the cheese?"

"Sure did."

"How about my medicine?"

"Got it right here."

"Is Ruthie aboard?"

"Yep. She's around somewheres."

Captain Dize, burly and weatherbeaten, told me, "Every trip I do errands for people—buy their medicine, their clothing, shoes; I even take their money to the bank. Don't charge for things like that; just freight."

On Monday, rain, shine, or blow, Frank Dize takes some 25 teen-agers to Crisfield to attend high school, and on Friday evening he brings them home.

At 5 p.m., right on schedule, the Daniel brothers and the Willens family arrived in their boats and rafted up alongside *Andromeda*. We had an important appointment—for a typical Chesapeake Bay dinner at the home of Mrs. Frances Kitching. If boatmen give her a few hours' notice, Mrs. Kitching will put before them a meal they'll never forget.

And she did for all of us. Fried chicken, ham, crab cakes, cole slaw, potato salad, corn pudding, oysters, applesauce, cucumbers, green beans—a Kitching meal goes on and on, ending with cake, pie, and coffee.

*S*mith Island has no doctor; none will live there. But it does have Schim Becker, a young Australian nurse who came to Baltimore to marry an Australian physician and instead married an artist and moved to Smith. The church pays her salary.

"I knew nothing about Smith Island before I came here," Schim said as we lounged on *Andromeda*'s deck. "But I like these people. As individuals they're egocentric. But they've learned through experience and their life on the water how to coexist. They dovetail beautifully."

Schim sends cases she can't handle to Crisfield by boat. In emergencies she summons a Navy helicopter. "But minor procedures I do myself. With telephone help from mainland doctors, I've relocated shoulders and made some difficult diagnoses."

I asked whether she was ever lonely in so isolated a spot. Schim shook her head emphatically. "I feel very happy with what I've achieved. Here I'm needed. And here I'm free—free from city pressures."

Our departure next morning was enlivened for onlookers when the Willenses went hard aground in the tricky channel. Bill heaved a line to them from *Andromeda*'s stern, and our hefty diesel worked them clear. So, in weather that looked dirty—though it never rained or blew more than 15 knots—both boats sailed a southerly course to Tangier Island in Virginia waters.

Progress had come to that small isle. On one side of the harbor

Watery main street winds past the town of Ewell, Maryland, on Smith Island— actually a cluster of marshy islands. Don Bradshaw can't keep a straight face for the photographer during class in Tylerton, another village on the island. Older children ride in Ullie Marshall's "school boat" from Tylerton to Rhodes Point, where a bus takes them on to Ewell. After eighth grade, students take another boat to high school on the mainland.

stretched a new, L-shaped bulkhead topped by a sign bearing the elegant words, "Yacht Parking." So we didn't berth *Andromeda*, we parked her, right behind the 35-foot sloop *Foregone*, whose skipper helped with our lines. In that manner we met two more Waterway gypsies, Winthrop Young, a retired FBI agent, and his wife, Celeste, from Cincinnati. They had sold their home and were living aboard *Foregone*. In a year and a half they had sailed the Great Lakes, made their way leisurely from Chicago to Cairo, Illinois, and on down the Mississippi, cruised the Gulf of Mexico, and then had traversed the Intracoastal Waterway from Key West to the Chesapeake.

"I've always wanted to cruise like this and do it while I still had my health," said Young, a giant of a man. "I was raised in New Haven, Connecticut, and learned sailing there. When other boys were throwing a baseball, I was fitting out a raft. My ancestors were whalers out of Rhode Island, and that tradition has always powerfully affected me."

Walking about Tangier, I found its terrain, its houses, its people looked very much like those of Smith Island. But there are differences. Tangier has a high school, and it has a government headed by Mayor Alva W. Crockett. But at present it, too, lacks a doctor. "We do have a nurse, a woman born and raised right on this island," said Mayor Crockett. "That woman is extra good at pulling teeth."

*T*hat evening, with the Willenses and the Youngs, we enjoyed a fitting sequel to the memorable dinner on Smith Island. Mrs. Hilda Crockett, who takes in guests, boarders, and stray yachtsmen, served us a meal reminiscent of Mrs. Kitching's.

Strolling back to the boats, we said goodbye to our sailing companions, the Willenses, knowing only chance would converge our courses again. On the morrow they and the Youngs would cross the Chesapeake and cruise Virginia's Great Wicomico and Piankatank Rivers. We would head for Norfolk and the beginning of that long inland passage yachtsmen call, quite inaccurately, "the Ditch."

All night the wind blew hard out of the northeast, pinning *Andromeda* against the bulkhead, and rain rattled against our ports. By dawn the wind slackened, and we got under way, knowing we faced long hours in bad weather.

The rain continued most of the day. No foul-weather gear keeps rainwater from running down my neck, and under our jackets Bill and I wore Turkish towels like scarves.

Yet the wind continued moderate and out of the northeast, a favorable slant, and nothing dampened our spirits—not the rain, nor the spray we took aboard off Norfolk, nor the long haul through crowded Hampton Roads and up the Elizabeth River to a marina at Portsmouth. We knew the next day would bring a new adventure, a cruise in waters strange to us all but with a colorful and storied past: the Dismal Swamp Canal.

Rich catch of Atlantic menhaden rises to the surface in a purse seine off Tangier Island, Virginia. The two boats that spread the huge net now stand by while the mother ship John D. Deihl *draws it to the surface with its flip-flopping contents. Purse-seine fishing is legal in Virginia waters but not in Maryland.*

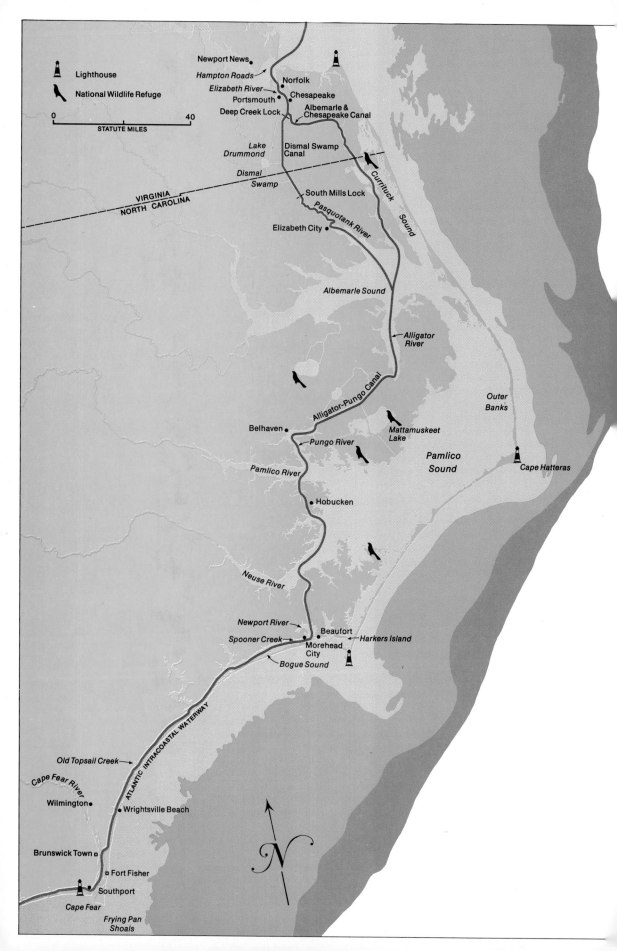

Lighthouse

National Wildlife Refuge

0 ——————— 40
STATUTE MILES

Newport News
Hampton Roads
Elizabeth River
Portsmouth
Deep Creek Lock
Norfolk
Chesapeake
Albemarle & Chesapeake Canal

Lake Drummond

Dismal Swamp Canal

Dismal Swamp

VIRGINIA
NORTH CAROLINA

South Mills Lock

Pasquotank River

Currituck Sound

Elizabeth City

Albemarle Sound

Alligator River

Alligator-Pungo Canal

Outer Banks

Belhaven
Pungo River

Mattamuskeet Lake

Pamlico River

Pamlico Sound

Cape Hatteras

Hobucken

Neuse River

Newport River
Spooner Creek
Beaufort
Harkers Island
Morehead City
Bogue Sound

ATLANTIC INTRACOASTAL WATERWAY

Old Topsail Creek

Cape Fear River

Wilmington
Wrightsville Beach

N

Brunswick Town
Fort Fisher

Southport
Cape Fear
Frying Pan Shoals

5

Southward Behind the Carolina Capes

*A*head, straight as a gun barrel, the still water of the Dismal Swamp Canal cut through walls of dark green as far as we could see. To *Andromeda*'s starboard maples, gums, poplars, pines, and oaks lined the Waterway in unbroken ranks. Many of their limbs bore clusters of mistletoe or long tentacles of Virginia creeper, and their trunks rose from impenetrable thickets of persimmon and myrtle. To port the trees grew as large but not as thickly, and occasionally we could glimpse a road paralleling the canal.

With no other boat in sight, we cruised slowly through an endless tunnel roofed by the sky. An intermittent sun, nearing its zenith, burnished a broad line down the middle of the canal, and rays broke through overhanging branches to spotlight sections of the embankments. Patches of reddening foliage flickered here and there but, on this last day of September, autumn had not yet touched many leaves.

Tranquillity and a dreamlike sense of solitude and remoteness enveloped boat and crew. Our bow cleaving that placid water, the gentle V of our wake, the low throb of the engine — these things seemed intrusive, and I cut the throttle back to little more than idling speed.

"A dull, monotonous place. . . ."

"Not much variety, not much to see."

That's the way two veteran Waterway travelers had described the Dismal Swamp Canal to me. But what a slander! That interplay of light and color and shadow monotonous? That prodigal verdure unvaried? The liquid call of a wood thrush, the swift blue flash of an indigo bunting, dull?

Virginia Finnegan gestured toward the thick foliage, then clasped her arms about her shoulders.

"Here nature embraces you," she said.

She had put it well. Not only tree and vine but sky and water,

Often called "the Big Ditch" from Norfolk, Virginia, southward, the Intracoastal Waterway traverses a protected course by way of rivers, canals, sounds, and dredged land cuts.

sun and shadow, reached out to include us in their gentle intermingling.

The "Great Dismal Swamp." Col. William Byrd II of colonial Virginia gave it that gross misnomer. In 1728 the Crown commissioned Byrd to chart a dividing line between Virginia and North Carolina, an exhausting task that took surveyors through the heart of the swamp. The colonel described it as "this vast body of dirt and nastiness."

Another notable surveyor saw the swamp quite differently. George Washington, who led a group into it in 1763 and made a number of subsequent visits, called it "a glorious paradise" abounding in wild fowl and game. He and several associates tried to drain part of the swamp in a lumbering venture.

Since then much of it has been drained, but it still covers some 210,000 acres, almost equally divided between Virginia and North Carolina. It is really a vast peat bog, and at its heart lies Lake Drummond, ringed by gaunt cypresses and dense forest. That secluded lake was our destination. We would reach it in a smaller boat through the 3½-mile "feeder ditch" that drains water from Lake Drummond into the canal.

*L*eaving Portsmouth in the early morning, we had motored up the Southern Branch of the Elizabeth River in gusty, threatening weather. Seven miles upstream from Portsmouth, the cruising boatman faces a choice. To starboard Deep Creek leads to the Dismal Swamp Canal. The Elizabeth's Southern Branch continues to the Albemarle and Chesapeake Canal, an alternate Waterway route. The two routes converge 70 miles farther south in the middle of Albemarle Sound.

We made the starboard turn and followed Deep Creek 2½ miles to a lock. Gates swung shut behind, water gushed into the basin, and we began a surprisingly swift 12-foot rise. Then, ahead, other gates opened and the lockmaster cast off our lines. We moved out, and in clearing weather entered the swamp.

Actually the canal parallels the eastern edge of the Great Dismal. Land to port, where we saw the road, had been reclaimed years before. But to starboard the shadowy tangle of the swamp, a living wall, rose higher than our mast.

Three boats that had shared the lock with us gradually melted from view. Apparently they intended to hurry through the swamp, as if fearful of the ghosts of runaway slaves who once lived there. Wielding pick and shovel, slaves dug most of the original canal, a ditch 22 miles long, 11 feet wide, and 2 feet deep. Work began in 1793, and by 1805 narrow, flat-bottom boats could traverse the entire length. I wondered how many men had been broken, how many had died, building the route yachtsmen now so blithely traveled.

Bill Gay, at the helm, brought me back to the present: "I'm having to stay near the middle to keep our mast and spreaders out of overhanging trees!"

Past cypress and pine, Andromeda glides along the Pasquotank River south of the Dismal Swamp Canal, one of America's oldest artificial waterways still in use. The Intracoastal route follows the river for 31 miles, from Turners Cut to Albemarle Sound.

Rail and highway bridges on the Southern Branch of the Elizabeth River open for a Liberian tanker carrying oil to the Port of Hampton Roads, Virginia, a vast natural harbor with facilities at Norfolk, Portsmouth, Chesapeake, and Newport News. In 1972 Hampton Roads handled 46 million tons of cargo, surpassed only by the New York-New Jersey port complex. Volkswagens unloaded at Portsmouth await overland transport to distributors. The tugboat Huntington helps move an overhauled tanker from its berth at Newport News Shipbuilding and Drydock.

At 11 o'clock we approached two small docks where *Ange's Angel,* a 29-foot powerboat, waited for us.

Jack Ange, owner and skipper of *Ange's Angel,* is one of my favorite characters. A rugged bear of a man, with a piratical-looking beard and the amiability that so often characterizes big men, Jack leisurely cruises and explores the southern part of the Waterway. He was a plumbing contractor until he fell in love with boating; then he retired and took to the water for much of the year.

On this day he had aboard his boat a baker's dozen of family and friends, among them his wife, Ruth, and Virginia Finnegan's husband. Maurice Finnegan would join us aboard *Andromeda* for a week. But now everyone piled aboard *Ange's Angel,* and Jack headed up the 30-foot-wide feeder ditch that cut into the swamp at right angles to the canal.

*B*ranches slapped at the boat's sides and in some places formed archways that had to be lifted or pushed aside by passengers crouched on the bow. Our skipper took it slow and steady, while keeping a wary eye ahead for snags.

We pushed on through the enfolding wilderness for three miles, finally tying up at a dock below a spillway and small dam. From that point outboard boats could be moved on a marine railway around the dam to another ditch leading to the lake. *Ange's Angel* bulked too large for such a portage, but Dewey Howell, the man who would show us Lake Drummond, waited atop the dam with two small boats. Six generations of his family have hunted in the depths of the Dismal Swamp. Dewey had agreed to let us stay overnight at his Lady of the Lake Lodge.

We didn't know it at the time, but our group would be among the last to visit that rustic hunting retreat. Union Camp Corporation, a timber company, soon would deed 50,000 acres of the swamp, including Lake Drummond, to the Nature Conservancy, and it in turn would give the property to the U. S. Department of the Interior for a wildlife refuge.

We cruised briefly down the ditch leading to the lake, then emerged from woodland so abruptly it seemed as if a wall between us and the rest of the world had suddenly been breached. Ahead lay a vast expanse of water, topped with whitecaps, that extended to distant wooded shores. Near us the snaggly black teeth of cypress stumps rose from the shallow water, and farther offshore old cypresses, still living but worn and derelict-looking, lifted grotesque limbs. Wisps of Spanish moss clung to some of them.

I commented on the color of the water; it looked like strong tea. "Tannic acid from juniper and cypress," Dewey said. "But it's good water to drink. In the old days many sailing ships carried it because it wouldn't spoil."

Unlike most lakes, Drummond has no tributaries; it is supplied by springs, artesian wells, and rainfall. The lake lies 18 feet above sea level, and its waters flow underground through spongy peat that supports the trackless forests.

In the sheltered ditches we hadn't realized the force of the wind, and our boat pounded severely through the whitecaps as we ran across the lake under gray skies to the far shore. But Dewey soon docked us at Lady of the Lake Lodge, a frame building darkly stained by weather. Sitting above the water on sturdy pilings, it contained several bedrooms, a kitchen, and a living-dining room, all simply furnished.

Our host led me behind the building to some large pens at the edge of the forest. They held dozens of hounds, and many bayed and yapped at the sight of Dewey.

"I like a good deep bass voice in a hound, or a real fine-mouthed dog that sounds excited all the time," he said. "You can only hunt deer in this swamp with the help of hounds. That growth is too thick for a man afoot, and it's right easy to get lost. We station hunters along the logging roads and drainage ditches, and the hounds drive the deer past 'em."

When we returned to the lodge, a huge meal had been laid out: Smithfield ham, cold roast beef, sliced tomatoes, corn on the cob, cherry pie, cupcakes, biscuits, rolls. To my surprise I saw that everyone had a slab of wood for a plate.

"We brought cedar shingles," said Virginia. "On Saturday, July 11, 1829, President Andrew Jackson rode the Dismal Swamp Canal on an inspection trip, and everyone ate a picnic lunch off shingles. I thought we should commemorate that event. If shingles were good enough for Andy Jackson, they're good enough for us."

Torrent of grain streams into a barge from a Belhaven, North Carolina, elevator. Life-jacketed Fred McCloud supervises the loading of 50,000 bushels—part of 3 million tons of commodities transported on the Waterway in North Carolina each year.

After dinner I sought the quiet of the dock. The wind had died, and the lowering skies had broken, permitting the sun to suffuse great masses of clouds with crimson. The dark waters reddened, then faithfully mirrored a lingering gold as the sun dropped below the horizon. Dusk stole across the waters, and it was night.

In 1803 the Irish poet Thomas Moore saw night come to Lake Drummond, and he wrote a poem based upon an Indian legend. His verses tell the story of a young man so crazed by grief at the death of his beloved that he thought she had fled from

Canoeists paddle shoreward at sundown on Lake Drummond, heart of the Dismal Swamp. A bald cypress (opposite), draped with Spanish moss, lifts its knees above waters stained by vegetation. In autumn, *Vaccinium* berries ripen among stands of timber. Drained and logged since colonial times for farming, lumbering, and commercial development, the swamp today encompasses about 330 square miles — a third of its area two centuries ago. In 1973 the Nature Conservancy acquired 78 square miles, including the lake, and then deeded the tract to the Government for management as a wildlife refuge.

131

her grave into the swamp, and he pursued her there, to be reunited at his own death:

> But oft, from the Indian hunter's camp,
> This lover and maid so true
> Are seen at the hour of midnight damp
> To cross the Lake by a fire-fly lamp,
> And paddle their white canoe!

In the clear, crisp air of morning we walked a logging road to Washington Ditch, a canal originally dug—also by slave labor—for George Washington and his associates. Union Camp had enlarged and maintained it. A nearby sign commemorated Washington's survey of 1763, and another marked the site where George's brother John built a shelter.

Water in the ditch looked dark as India ink, but it was not stagnant. That canal and others like it had been draining the area slowly for years, and Lake Drummond's waters, once 11 to 12 feet deep, now measured 5 to 6 feet in most places.

Upon our return to *Andromeda* that evening, I sat long in the cockpit while a cold dew settled and the hours of darkness passed. All my life I have been a night person, soothed by shadow, my spirits lifted by stars. That night the viewing fulfilled the clear promise of the day, and my special constellation, Andromeda, rose overhead in the corridor formed by the trees.

Andromeda, the beautiful Chained Lady of mythology. Her own father, King of Ethiopia, chained her to a rock in the sea to appease the wrath of a devouring monster. But Perseus killed the monster, freed Andromeda, and married her. After her death she was transported to the sky, where, luminous and lovely, she glows for all to see.

I stared fixedly at Andromeda's waist, opposite the constellation Triangulum. Yes, I could see it!—a faint, hazy smudge of light, the Great Nebula in Andromeda, a spiral galaxy like the Milky Way and the most distant object visible to the naked eye.

When sailing, I too am released from bonds, I too know a soaring escape. And a glimpse of that swirling cluster of worlds beyond worlds, however faint, has always been for me so humbling and so moving that it seems to cleanse my soul.

So my sailboats have been *Andromeda,* for me the epitome of freedom—and the other woman in my life.

The next day we motored leisurely down the remainder of the Dismal Swamp Canal, passing into North Carolina waters.

At South Mills, one of two locks on the Dismal Swamp Canal, William Brickhouse helps secure a northbound yacht before releasing 1¼ million gallons of water to raise the boat to the canal's level. His off-duty colleague, Andrew Pearce, talks about a different—and favorite—subject: the local swamp honey (in the jar on the table), made from persimmon nectar.

On the winding Pasquotank River, timeless meeting place of woodland and water, each bend revealed yet another vista of wild solitude, with tall cypresses and pines growing along both shores. Not until the river widened near Elizabeth City did we see houses. The Pasquotank stands out in my mind for its splendid isolation. In one respect cruising an unspoiled river is not unlike sailing the ocean: The remoteness and silence are balm. But on the Pasquotank, as so often on the rivers of the Chesapeake, I asked myself, "Can this beauty last?"

Just before dusk we pulled into the Elizabeth City Shipyard and Marina, a big but quiet facility with the intimate and friendly air of a club. To our surprise and pleasure we spied *Nevermore*, last seen in New Jersey waters, lying at a nearby pier, and we renewed acquaintance with Gene Hebert and his family. They had been plagued with engine trouble. Next day the Willenses, our companions at Smith and Tangier Islands, arrived in *Lanikai* and reported a pleasant conclusion of their Chesapeake cruise.

*E*lizabeth City is the gateway to North Carolina's Albemarle, Currituck, and Pamlico Sounds, those big but shallow bodies of water lying behind the Outer Banks and Cape Hatteras. Residents call the huge area Sounds Country. Little developed, sparsely populated, it is more a place of water than of land, and many of its sandspits and wooded shores seem to exist only because of the grudging tolerance of wind and wave.

A trading center with many handsome residences, Elizabeth City is not only the gateway but the metropolis of Sounds Country. Yet the community contains only 15,000 people, and growth has been slow. A lot of people like it that way.

I began to understand why as I kept running into local people on the waterfront. Everyone seemed relaxed, open, convivial. A storekeeper and a mechanic both told me they should be working but preferred watching boats. An elderly man said he had come down to the waterfront to look at the site for a proposed municipal park. Businessman Phil Sawyer invited me aboard one of the handsomest old houseboat-cruisers I have ever seen, the 77-foot *Southern Belle V*, now a grande dame 44 years old. In spring and fall, Phil and his wife, Isabelle, forsake their house and live aboard their boat at the marina so they can meet Waterway gypsies.

But Curtis Olds, who works on the waterfront, may have been the most relaxed person I met. A retired Coast Guard chief warrant officer, he had just begun a sight-seeing service on the Pasquotank with *Leah*, a 50-foot converted Navy launch. Business was still slow, however, and Curtis had leisure to yarn with passersby or to go out on the river just for fun.

"The dawn, that's my time," he said. "I like to hear the swamp come awake—a wood thrush, a squirrel chattering. Just nature itself."

On the evening of our second day at Elizabeth City, driving rain and gusty winds enveloped the entire area. The foul weather continued for several days, and before it abated the Finnegans had to return home.

At last the wind moderated and hauled around to the northwest, promising wind and seas astern as we crossed Albemarle Sound. So we got under way down the Pasquotank and pushed out into open water.

Notorious Albemarle Sound. Many experienced boatmen think it the roughest, most treacherous body of water on the entire Atlantic Intracoastal route. Here the seas often become highly unpredictable, and the waves take on a steepness not always warranted by the strength of the wind.

As we began our crossing, the breeze was about 10 knots, but the water seemed to us much rougher than it should have been in such air. Lines of froth streaked the surface in a manner we associated with considerably stronger winds. By the time we reached the broad mouth of the Alligator River, the wind velocity had picked up to nearly 20 knots, and *Andromeda* pitched and rolled under power. We crossed an area where the chart showed only seven feet of water, and I wondered if we would slam our keel on the bottom while in the trough of a wave.

I have heard and read many technical reasons for Albemarle Sound's roughness, but the most concise and lucid explanation was given me by a professional yacht captain and Waterway veteran, Henning Nielsen, of Boston and Miami Springs:

"It's fresh water, and it's shallow, and it's big enough for the winds to get a good fetch. These factors produce closely packed waves, with not much distance between them, and in such cases they are always steep. The result is a confused sea, with the waves unable to establish a pattern."

In the Alligator River we sailed protected waters, with cypress swamps on either side and not a sign of habitation. Again *Andromeda*'s crew expressed surprise and pleasure at how much of the Waterway remained wilderness country. In the afternoon we entered a long but desolate cut with banks as straight as parallel rules, and finally emerged into the Pungo River. There we tied up at Belhaven in a little harbor huddling behind a low and inadequate breakwater.

Down the waterfront I had glimpsed a ship with four tall masts, and I walked along the shore until I found her alongside an old bulkhead. Soon I stood on the deck of the most bizarre

Pet mynah perched on his hand, Mayor Axson Smith of Belhaven supervises a buffet dinner at his River Forest Manor, a resort on the Pungo River. Yachtsmen and their guests choose from such dishes as fried trout, shrimp creole, oyster fritters, and crab casserole.

Waterway vagabond with no schedule to meet steers his sloop-rigged sailboat toward Morehead City, North Carolina. Families and retired couples, honeymooners and loners cruise the Inland Waterway in craft ranging from 100-foot "gold-platers" to small runabouts; says a veteran, "Eventually you see almost anything that will float." During the annual fall migration from northern waters to Florida, a two-masted yacht and several power cruisers pass in convoy through the Alligator-Pungo Canal.

ship I have ever seen, and talked to one of the most singular men I have ever encountered.

The *W. J. Eckert* was an ugly duckling. Stain and rust spotted her unpainted metal hull. Oil drums cut in half and fitted into the deck served as hatches. The rough wooden masts looked as if they had been hewn with stone axes. The ship had no yard-arms or running rigging. Though 98 feet long, she had a beam of only 14 feet—no wider than *Andromeda*—so that she seemed skinny as a fence rail. When the wind gusted to about 15 knots, I could feel her heel over.

Her owner and master, T. S. Applegate, a diminutive man with shaggy, untrimmed beard and hair and greasy coveralls, talked about the *Eckert* in a pleasant, cultivated voice.

"I began building her in 1967 in Lynchburg, Virginia, during a Christmas vacation," he said, "but I started work on the design in 1964. I think my son Jesse and I will finish her this year or next."

Applegate told me that he had taught physics and chemistry, had skippered a three-masted schooner in the Hawaiian Islands, and had a master-of-sail license. He said he had finally finished the steel hull in 1970, then had it hauled from Lynchburg to the Western Branch of the Elizabeth River for launching. Later he brought it to Belhaven.

He and Jesse, a taller version of his father, including beard and blackened coveralls, were now "finishing" the boat. Yet when I squeezed down a hatch I found the interior a maze of raw metal bulkheads. Father and son slept on wooden platforms, and there were no heads.

Why had he attempted this lonely, difficult task?

"I thought that if I could provide my family any kind of opportunity, it would be sea experience," he said. And that was his only reply.

What would he do with his ship?

"I've thought about charter work in the Caribbean, where the people aren't so particular about accommodations," he said. Later, however, he told me he thought he would sail to the Cape Verde Islands off the west coast of Africa.

I waved goodbye to that driven but likable man, and he turned again to his work and his long, long dream.

We left for Morehead City in bright blue weather, but with the wind blowing 15 to 20 knots out of the northeast. That didn't concern me at the time, since we had the wind on our stern, and the seas didn't bother us in either the Pungo or Pamlico Rivers, both broad. Later on, however, I knew we would have to push out into the wide mouth of the Neuse River, and there the winds would take us on the beam after a long fetch down Pamlico Sound. My friend Capt. Roy Jenkins, the Waterway expert, had told me not to go out in the Neuse in a northeast wind of more than 12 knots.

Frankly I thought that a bit conservative, and after Hobucken Bridge I ignored my friend's advice and took *Andromeda* into the river under power. The water was a sea of white, not blue, and we rolled uncomfortably. Minutes later we lost all protection from the shore, and the wind picked up to 25 knots. Now *Andromeda* pitched and rolled wildly, and I looked down the hatchway and saw Mike lying spread-eagled on the cabin sole, unable to stand or even sit, while plastic glasses and cups, apples, grapefruit, books, flashlights —all the objects not securely stowed in the galley or on bulkhead shelves —flew around her. Bill lurched below and helped get things in order.

Roy had been right, as usual. Pamlico Sound behaves much like Albemarle, with steep, confused seas any time a sustained wind exceeds 12 knots out of the northeast.

Finally we worked our way to a position where we could turn up the Neuse and take the winds astern for a much easier ride. Once out of the river we cruised protected waters all the way past Morehead City to Spooner Creek, its modern marina a very welcome haven for a tired crew.

We thought Morehead City un-attractive, but Beaufort, a community just across the Newport River, is a colonial jewel founded in 1709, nearly a century and a half before Morehead City. Beaufort's shady streets offer the stroller 25 houses built before the Revolution and more than a hundred that predate the Civil War. Ship carpenters built some of the houses in the waterfront area, and the close-fitting excellence of their handiwork remains evident.

Resuming our cruise the next morning, we motored down a dredged channel in broad but shallow Bogue Sound, passing dozens of "disposal" islands built up from silty sand lifted by the dredges and already rich in bird life.

After Bogue Sound we ran through a long succession of land cuts and dredged paths behind banks and sandspits adjoining the ocean. On our port side natural inlets often linked the Water-way to the sea, and to starboard we passed many summer cottages, usually rather stark and ugly. This section of the Waterway seemed the least attractive we had traveled.

Yet it, too, had its touch of beauty. From Virginia south we

Blue crab undergoes monitoring of its blood conductivity at the Atlantic Estuarine Fisheries Center, Beaufort. Biologist David Engel adjusts an antenna that receives signals from a transmitter in the crab's back. Data plotted on the console shows how the crab adapts to sudden changes in water salinity.

had noticed many large bushes bearing what appeared to be white blossoms, and along North Carolina's part of the Waterway these bushes at times grew as profusely as flower borders along a walk. The woody plants were sea myrtle, their "flowers" fluffy seeds like the down of the dandelion.

At Wrightsville Beach near Wilmington, North Carolina, we tarried three days for the most varied sight-seeing of our entire voyage. This area adjoining the Cape Fear River contains many attractions that should not be bypassed: three of the South's finest gardens, Greenfield, Airlie, and Orton; the carefully preserved ruins of Brunswick Town, founded in 1726 but abandoned half a century later when the British invaded the Cape Fear River; the battleship *North Carolina*, now a war memorial, where Mike, descending to an engine room, said she felt as though we were crawling through the entrails of a dinosaur.

But, most of all, we enjoyed exploring the area's intimate associations with the Civil War. In the waning days of the Confederacy in 1865, the port of Wilmington alone remained open to blockade runners. Two bastions on the Cape Fear River, Fort Fisher and Fort Anderson, held off Federal gunboats.

Both forts were earthen, and today only their hilly contours, softened by time, remain. But at each site North Carolina has assembled fascinating dioramas and other materials telling the stories of these redoubts.

In December 1864, Fort Fisher repelled a heavy attack by Union ships and troops. But the following January the North mounted the greatest naval bombardment and amphibious attack the world had yet seen, with 60 ships and 8,000 men. Invaders breached the defenses, and the fort fell after bloody hand-to-hand fighting. Anderson held out 35 days longer.

Near Fort Fisher the Blockade Runner Museum tells the story of the fast ships and the wily crews that attempted to slip through the Federal fleet off the Cape Fear River. Of 2,054 runs of the blockade attempted by Confederate and British-owned ships in the Carolinas, 1,735 — 84 percent — were successful!

*O*ur next stop, Southport, the last port of call in North Carolina, was some 20 miles distant, but we began the run early in the morning because high winds and rain were expected later. They never materialized, and we enjoyed a very pleasant sail across the wide Cape Fear River. Trawlers worked their seines along our route, and great flocks of gulls flapped erratically off the sterns of the fishing boats, sounding their high-pitched quarrelsome cry and diving for fish.

Our destination of Southport brought to mind the Plummers, those doughty heroes of *The Boy, Me and the Cat*. In 1912 no Waterway ran between Beaufort and Southport, and the Plummers took to the sea, hoping to slip behind Frying Pan Shoals in good weather and get into the Cape Fear River. But a storm forced them to seek sanctuary in an inlet, and there they went

Bounty of North Carolina's
coastal waters forms a still
life at a Morehead City fish
market. Clockwise from the
22-pound lobster: clams,
shrimp, blue crabs, more
clams, speckled trout, mullet,
oysters, and bluefish. The
state's commercial fisheries
landed 168 million pounds of
seafood in 1972; most species
caught spend part of their
life cycles in the vast estuarine system protected by the
Outer Banks. At left, a sunrise fisherman casts for bluefish and drum in the surf
at Wrightsville Beach.

hard aground, their catboat and launch suffering severe damage before father and son could get them inshore.

For more than a week, with no protection from wind and cold, they worked feverishly at repairs. Henry, Sr., wrote in his log:

"December 13-20. During these days we were marooned at New Inlet, as desolate a spot on our Atlantic coast as a man could pick out for the purpose. The fear of a northeast gale with heavy sea was constantly on our minds for that might easily spell imprisonment for days if not weeks. We lay in a narrow little gutter where the tide ran viciously, making constant shifting of anchors both night and day a necessity. I must utterly fail to give any idea of the great loneliness of the beach stretching 1000 miles on either side and trembling to the constant crash of the roaring surf."

But eventually they made their two craft watertight and sailed to Southport, where they enjoyed a comfortable Christmas.

*N*orth Carolina, like New Jersey, has gotten into the marina business, and at Southport we took a slip in a quiet state-owned facility. But late that night Mike got me awake to report something disturbing. "There's a strange noise in *Andromeda*'s bilge," she said. "I never heard anything like it before."

Scotty, the Plummers' cat, probably never slept as lightly as my wife does aboard a boat. Once before she had awakened me to identify a noise in the bilge. It turned out to be the sound of our propeller revolving in a racing ebb tide.

But this time she had heard something I couldn't explain. After crawling into the engine room, I could hear the sound plainly: a gritty, continuous snapping and crackling that seemed to come from the hull all about me. A flashlight revealed nothing, and I got Bill awake to listen. He too was puzzled. We crawled through the boat, hearing the noise forward and aft. It seemed to be in the hull below the waterline; for a moment I thought perhaps the fiberglass was cracking and crazing.

Then a memory glimmered, and I went into the after cabin and took from a shelf the January 1958 issue of NATIONAL GEOGRAPHIC. Its lead article, "Slow Boat to Florida," described a trip down the Intracoastal Waterway by my old friends Dorothea and Stuart E. Jones. I thumbed through it. Yes, there, on page 61 — they had heard the same sound at Fernandina Beach, Florida, and had finally attributed it to fish feeding upon growth on the hull, and shrimp snapping their claws while swarming around dock pilings. The hull, a kind of drum, amplified the noises that these creatures made.

"You should write Stu and Dorothea and thank them for solving our mystery," Mike said.

"I'll give them a copy of the book and let them read about it," I replied.

So, with the strange cacophony still continuing, we drifted off to sleep.

In his backyard workshop, 91-year-old Stacy F. Guthrie of Harkers Island needs a month of fine weather to build a fishing boat. As a 17-foot boat nears completion, he tightens a set-screw on his old band saw, holds a deckframe piece in place with a C-clamp, and trims a board for the motor well. A retired fisherman, Mr. Guthrie began making boats full-time after World War II "to have something to do."

Nesting refuges for wildfowl, "disposal" islands formed by 40 years of dredging line the Waterway nort

Wrightsville Beach. Old Topsail Creek cuts between them (top to center); Old Point lies at lower left.

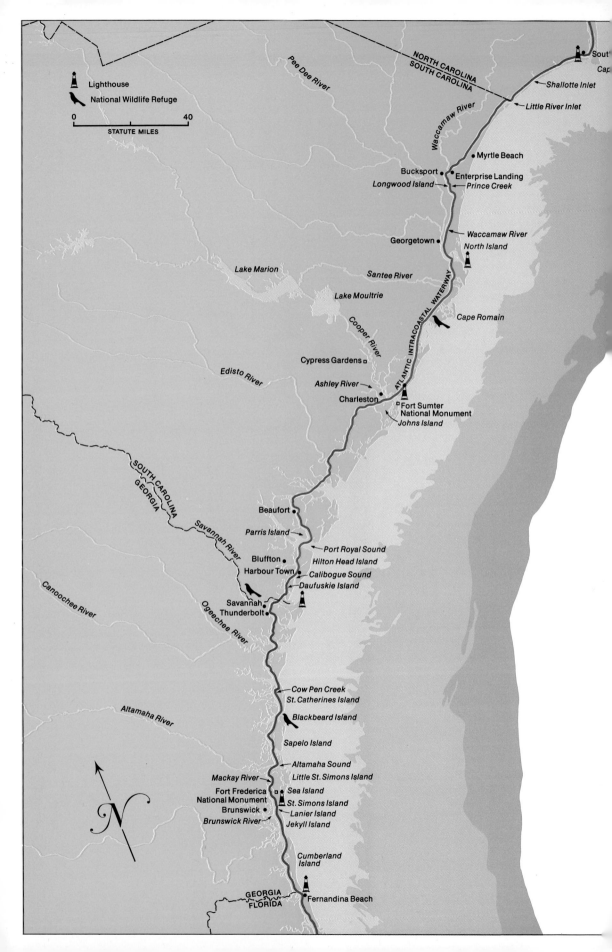

Lighthouse

National Wildlife Refuge

0   STATUTE MILES   40

NORTH CAROLINA
SOUTH CAROLINA

Pee Dee River

Waccamaw River

Sout
Cap

← Shallotte Inlet

← Little River Inlet

● Myrtle Beach

Bucksport ●
Longwood Island ●   ● Enterprise Landing
                    ← Prince Creek

Georgetown ●   ← Waccamaw River
              North Island

Lake Marion

Santee River

Lake Moultrie

Cooper River

ATLANTIC INTRACOASTAL WATERWAY

Cape Romain

Edisto River

Cypress Gardens □

Ashley River →

Charleston ●
□ Fort Sumter
National Monument

Johns Island

SOUTH CAROLINA
GEORGIA

Savannah River

Beaufort ●

Parris Island →

Port Royal Sound
Hilton Head Island

Bluffton ●
Harbour Town ●   ← Calibogue Sound
                 ← Daufuskie Island

Canoochee River

Savannah ●
Thunderbolt ●

Ogeechee River

Altamaha River

← Cow Pen Creek
St. Catherines Island

Blackbeard Island

Sapelo Island

← Altamaha Sound

Mackay River →   Little St. Simons Island
Fort Frederica   Sea Island
National Monument □
Brunswick ●   ← St. Simons Island
Brunswick River → Lanier Island
                 Jekyll Island

Cumberland
Island

N

GEORGIA
FLORIDA   Fernandina Beach

6

Golden Days Among the Golden Isles

"*O*ctober 19—Had intended to remain at Southport, since rain and high winds were forecast. However, decided to leave when the forecast changed and the day dawned sunny and warm. We got under way at 0915 hours, and now, at 1015, the sky is overcast and more threatening-looking every mile south."

So began my morning log entry on the day we put North Carolina waters behind us and entered South Carolina, bound for Bucksport. It proved to be a day of sharp contrasts: The weather rapidly deteriorated; on the other hand, the appearance of the Waterway—rather drear most of the way—dramatically improved as we neared our destination.

A falling barometer did not surprise us, but the thermometer also dropped—and then dropped more and more and more. At Southport the temperature had been a pleasant 69, but by late afternoon it had plummeted to 41. In the open cockpit of *Andromeda* the wind-chill factor added to our discomfort. I put on a sweat shirt, later added a jacket, and still later donned foul-weather gear. Mike went below, and Bill, who seldom made any concession to chilly weather, put on a heavy wool sweater.

During the morning we ran much of the time through land cuts; off to port, beyond sandbanks and marshes, we could see large summer homes on dunes overlooking the ocean. At Shallotte Inlet a dredge sucked mud out of the Waterway and spewed it onto huge mounds. With the tide out, the inlet was a vast expanse of compact sand. Distantly, where sand met sea, breakers lashed at Shallotte's door.

Near Little River Inlet we entered South Carolina and began a long run through Pine Island Cut, well inland from the ocean. We moved along through high embankments, scraggly woods, and dirty water. Occasionally Bill dodged floating logs, but most of the time he steered lazily with his feet along a route as straight as our mast while I napped in the cockpit.

After transiting a scenic section of the Waccamaw River, the Waterway continues to Charleston. From there it twists through the Sea Islands and marshlands of South Carolina and Georgia.

As if on cue, I awakened and Mike came topside when *Andromeda* entered the Waccamaw River at Enterprise Landing. Since the time of the Indians, boatmen have been groping for superlatives to describe the Waccamaw. Many believe it to be the loveliest part of the southern Waterway.

On either side of *Andromeda* huge cypresses rose on crooked legs. Each limb held its burden of pendant moss, a gray veil behind which the forest brooded in stillness and shadow. With the sky heavily overcast, the water looked black as onyx, and it spread out beneath the trees in quiet, half-seen pools where lush green thickets grew.

Spanish moss, perhaps because of its somber monochrome, often induces in me a vague melancholy, not unpleasant, and I muse about the past. I find the mood rather like an autumnal reverie when the sere and yellow bring to mind the lost years and the old dreams. For long minutes I succumbed to that spell, rousing myself only when we approached Bucksport.

The best of the Waccamaw still lay ahead of us. Anything so beautiful should be shared, and at Bucksport we would be joined by two old friends from college years, Dave and Libbie Johnson of Princeton, New Jersey.

Bucksport isn't really a town; it's a country store, a little restaurant, and several houses set high and dry on solid ground that commands a sweeping bend of the river. A long, solidly built wharf hugs the shoreline, and there we tied up.

That night the temperature fell to 36°, and the wind strummed *Andromeda*'s rigging unceasingly. On the second night the thermometer got as low as 38, and the wind continued. But we had warm sleeping bags and electric heaters.

*A*t twilight of the second day I happened to be strolling the wharf alone when a battered old sailboat powered by a little outboard motor approached. At the helm sat a shaggy-haired man who wore only shorts and a T-shirt, despite the chill. He had a hard, chiseled face, and tattoos decorated his arms. He steered with his bare feet, and in his arms he cradled an old single-barreled shotgun.

I stared at him, he stared at me. I waved tentatively, he nodded almost imperceptibly. Without a word he went slowly past and continued down the river.

Once that strange apparition had disappeared around a bend, I almost believed I had dreamed the incident. But later, at Charleston, I met people who had encountered the man. He was a moody and eccentric Canadian. No one knew his name, but someone had dubbed him Smiling Sam because he never smiled. He had a reputation for brandishing his gun and shouting incoherently when a powerboat passed him throwing a rough wake.

I would have reason to recall Smiling Sam when we reached Hilton Head Island.

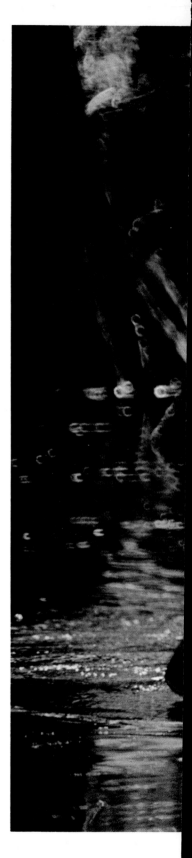

Gliding through shadowy lagoons, visitors tour Cypress Gardens by boat near Charleston, South Carolina.

Reminders of a past both gracious and turbulent, houses along South
Battery Street face the Charleston harbor. From upper-story piazzas
in 1861, residents witnessed the bombardment of Fort Sumter that
triggered the Civil War. Many years later author DuBose Heyward,
living in a house farther along this row, wrote the novel Porgy, on
which George Gershwin based the folk opera Porgy and Bess. About
1838 ironsmith Christopher Werner forged the Sword Gates that mark the
entrance to 32 Legare Street; two horizontal swords across four vertical
spears support the scrollwork. In 1751 planter William Branford built the
house at 59 Meeting Street, now the home of Mr. and Mrs. B. Owen
Geer, Jr. (right). Cypress paneling covers the walls throughout the
Georgian "double house," four main rooms with wide bisecting hallways.
Sadler tiles from Liverpool frame the raised grate of the living-room
fireplace; on the mantel stand antique Dresden vases and English plates.

The Johnsons had arrived on schedule from Princeton, so the next morning we lazed our way down the river. As if to make amends for the last two days, the sun soon warmed the air to the pleasant languor of Indian summer. The cypresses, now bathed with dappled light as well as dark water, lost much of their brooding look; and the moss took on just the suggestion of a delicate green. Atop old stumps and logs, turtles basked communally in the warmth; Mike counted a cluster of five, and Libbie soon topped her with nine.

I had a pleasant problem: where to anchor *Andromeda* so that we could explore by dinghy. The chart showed backwaters and tributaries in profusion. "They make great hurricane holes," Capt. Roy Jenkins, the Waterway veteran, had told me. "Run your boat up one of those creeks, tie up to some cypress trees, and you can ride out any blow."

Prince Creek, I noted, meandered off from the Waccamaw and rejoined it farther downstream, creating swampy Longwood Island. That island looked inviting. So we anchored off its southerly tip at the juncture of creek and river and launched our inflatable dinghy with its little two-horsepower motor.

Since the dinghy only held three people comfortably, I sent Libbie, Dave, and Bill off to reconnoiter for an hour while Mike and I kept an anchor watch. On their return I took Libbie's place, and we motored up Prince Creek, a thoroughfare broad enough for the passage of large craft.

At first the island seemed an almost solid wall of bushes; occasionally a break in the tangle led inward, only to end in yet another green impasse. But Dave and Bill had found one promising entry, and we poled into it with oars, pushing aside grass, vines, mulberry bushes, and strands of aptly named saw brier. Deeper and deeper we penetrated, until we began wondering if we could find our way out.

Then, to our delight, we parted some branches and broke out into an open pond with cottonwoods and reddening gums along its fringes, several tiny islets, and a profusion of luxuriant water plants. It seemed remarkably like a garden pool, lost and forgotten but still exquisite, and now ours by right of discovery.

At that moment some unseen creature plunged noisily into the pond, shattering my proprietary dream. The animal belonged there, we did not. You can't own Eden.

*G*eorgetown is a community with a split personality. On the one hand it's an industrial town, with a huge, noisome paper mill and a steel plant; yet it's also a charming legacy from the past, where "ante bellum" can mean pre-Revolutionary War homes as well as pre-Civil War. Some of these old dwellings date from Georgetown's heyday as the hub of a vast system of rice culture. Rice was grown here before 1700, and by 1840 the area produced nearly half the nation's crop.

Many trawlers work out of Georgetown, and from one of

Swinging among azaleas and dogwoods, 13-year-old Jane Maybank plays in the garden of her grandmother, Mrs. G. Kirkwood King, in Charleston. Many of the city's private gardens, cultivated to perfection over several generations, open their gates to the public for tours every spring.

Evening quiet settles over the boat-rimmed basin of Harbour Town, a marina at the resort o

a Pines Plantation on Hilton Head Island, South Carolina, just off the Intracoastal Waterway.

them we bought fresh shrimp. All hands aboard *Andromeda* helped with the cleaning, and then Mike prepared *scampi*. Fortunately, everyone agreed on the importance of garlic in the sauce; when the vote is unanimous, the question of social acceptability isn't even mentioned.

We departed for Charleston on a cool, misty morning, but the sun soon burned away the night vapors, bringing a resurgence of summer. Our dredged route took us through vast fields of thick marsh grass, part of the Cape Romain National Wildlife Refuge. When we had journeyed north with the spring, the grass of the southern marshes was a tender green; now it stretched away in golden undulations toward the distant ocean. Sky and grass, that's all our world consisted of; it reminded me of the savannas of East Africa, where an infinity of tawny oat grass meets the fathomless blue of the sky in wild loneliness.

Here we shared the Waterway with a prodigal assortment of bird life: gulls, white herons, great blue herons, hawks, terns, cormorants, flocks of redwing blackbirds. Frequently gulls and cormorants would wait until the last moment before avoiding our bow. The gulls rose lazily, but the cormorants dived and came up well astern. Both maneuvers seemed so practiced we wondered if this might be a familiar game the birds enjoyed.

With a flick of harvesting tongs, Andrew Kidd tosses oysters into his boat at low tide near Bluffton, South Carolina. Although Bluffton's marshes so far have remained open to oystermen, pollution spreading northward from the Savannah River has killed the once-thriving oyster business of nearby Daufuskie Island.

Charlestonians have sometimes referred to their proud old city as the place where the Cooper and Ashley Rivers meet to form the Atlantic. Their confluence does form a broad estuary, which *Andromeda* crossed in a spanking breeze. We motored past the Battery's high walls and on up the Ashley to the big municipal marina, protected by its own sea wall.

Almost any American associates the name "Charleston" with splendid old homes. Indeed, residents of the city have restored hundreds of vintage dwellings, and still the work goes on. Communities all over the country have modeled protective laws and zoning ordinances after those of Charleston.

Thomas E. Thornhill, president of the Historic Charleston Foundation, says the city can thank its former poverty for the extraordinary number of aged yet beautiful houses.

"For a long time after the Civil War, we were so destitute that we had to live in our old houses rather than tear them down and build something new," he told me. "Boston, New York, and many other cities went so far ahead of us economically that they could afford to replace many homes and buildings that now would be considered old gems worthy of preservation."

We walked the historic district carrying rented tape recorders that told us where to go and what to see. The residences ranged from great brick and stucco mansions along the Battery to little Federal-style row houses in hidden, unsuspected alleys with tiny formal gardens behind wrought-iron gates.

I considered journeying to Fort Sumter aboard *Andromeda,* but the surge around the shoal on which the fort sits had looked severe as we crossed the harbor. So we went there on *Beauregard,* a big sight-seeing boat. Ashore we explored all the parapets, battlements, and inner fastnesses of the huge, five-sided structure, now a national monument. Confederates accepted its surrender on April 14, 1861, and the South then held it against repeated heavy attacks for nearly four years.

Waterway gypsies who stop and tarry at the city's hospitable marina sooner or later meet that old salt Capt. George Lockwood, a retired tugboat operator who spends most of his waking hours at the marina store or on the porch of a nearby yacht club. Captain George, 75, bluff and vital with a nonstop, pell-mell manner of spinning a yarn, has known the southern Waterway since earliest childhood.

"Water rats, that's us," he says. "My grandfather was a blockade runner, and my father a tugboat captain pulling barges. As a boy I would sit on my dad's lap at night or stand on a box beside him and tell him how far offshore he was. I could see branches or the way the shoreline curved, but he couldn't.

"They didn't have markers on the Waterway until after 1918. We operated by memory and by knowing the way the ebb tides cut the channels. As for charts, we didn't believe in 'em."

On the morning of our departure from Charleston, Bill Gay brought me a hitchhiker. The young man said he was traveling the Waterway by kayak, but had been warned of open water south of Charleston and wanted us to take him and his little boat aboard *Andromeda.* I knew of no really dangerous water, but said we would take him to our next stop, Beaufort, South Carolina. He was tall and slender, with a pink-cheeked, handsome face, short blond hair, and a soft voice.

We hadn't been long under way before I realized there was something strange about our passenger. He never looked at any of us when speaking; instead, he seemed to gaze off into some private, remote world. When Dave Johnson attempted to include him in a photograph, he protested, saying an image on film drained and diminished him.

I will call him Jimmy, though that's not his name. He said he was from a western state, had been in military service, had finished two years of college, was divorced, and had a son. "I got all that over with," he said in a near whisper, as if his life to date, including marriage and fatherhood, had been something to hurry through compulsively and then dismiss.

"Why are you traveling the Waterway in a kayak?" I asked.

"I want to find out where my abilities lie," he said.

"If you mean the skills necessary to earn a living, you can't learn much paddling a kayak," I replied.

He considered my statement vaguely for a long moment and then, with numerous pauses, said, "I wanted to do something dangerous. I'm learning to survive.

"I needed something to strengthen my personality," he added. "Last year I tried walking from Monterey to San Diego. I only got a hundred miles. I couldn't stand the loneliness. This time I decided to put myself in a precarious position in strange territory. That way I couldn't run home very easily."

The speech was impressive, until I recalled Jimmy had said he obtained the kayak in New England but rode with it on a truck all the way to Georgetown, South Carolina. I pointed out he did not get any survival training on that truck.

He frowned slightly, as if weighing what I said.

"You're certainly in no danger hitching a ride on this boat," I added. "That doesn't mold your character. Why ride with us?"

Again he thought with painful slowness.

"That's to keep this journey fluid," he said.

For a moment I thought he was making a pun about water, but jokes were beyond him. At Beaufort he gave Bill a book to present to me. It proved a frightening book, but it told much about Jimmy. Written by a "swami," it extolled the mystic benefits of drugs, how they helped one attain a "fluid" life, the highest plane of living.

Poor, confused, slow-thinking Jimmy, talking in riddles, apparently a casualty of the drug culture. We helped him unload his kayak at Beaufort's municipal marina, and he sat beside it quietly, the otherworldly look again on his face.

There were tears in Mike's eyes. "Little boy lost," she whispered to me.

*B*ewfort. That's the way you pronounce the South Carolina city. The one in North Carolina is *Bo*fort. The South Carolinians proved wonderfully hospitable to *Andromeda*'s crew, and their Beaufort contained even more handsome old homes than the namesake city to the north.

Ever since the cold snap on the Waccamaw we had enjoyed warm, golden days, and the remarkably uniform weather continued as we set out for Hilton Head, one of the Sea Islands—the Golden Isles—that lie off the South Carolina and Georgia mainlands. Crossing broad Port Royal Sound, we were entertained by porpoises spouting and cavorting around *Andromeda*.

Patiently accepti

THOMAS NEBBIA

eir ox's slow gait, three boys ride past an abandoned church on sparsely populated Daufuskie Island.

Harbour Town on Hilton Head is the handsomest marina on the entire Waterway. Here people with talent, taste, and a great deal of money created an attractive little town designed to look like a Mediterranean village.

We arrived on Halloween. In Beaufort Dave had carved a jack-o'-lantern from a big pumpkin, and now we placed it on *Andromeda*'s bowsprit in a bed of Spanish moss where its crooked grin, snaggly teeth, and glaring eyes would best be displayed. After dark, with a big candle burning inside, it drew groups of appreciative onlookers, including some pint-size members of the "trick-or-treat" set.

Three companies have developed Hilton Head's 30,000 acres with homes, golf courses, and all the commercial amenities. Basically I do not like to see any wild and beautiful place developed, but on Hilton Head it has been done with concern for the ecology and natural scenery. This is particularly true of developer Charles Fraser, who has left beaches, tidal marshes, and woodland largely undisturbed.

Smallest member of the heron family, a least bittern hides in a thicket of reeds at the national wildlife refuge on Blackbeard Island, Georgia. Opposite, a labyrinth of twisting channels caused by the sea's continual invasion of coastal streams and rivers cuts through the marshes of St. Simons Island, Georgia. In the distance at upper right, the Intracoastal Waterway follows the Mackay River in a wide S-curve.

THOMAS NEBBIA (OPPOSITE)

A dinner conversation with this unusual man moved across the broad gamut of his interests, from Sea Islands history and the collecting of old maps to environmental problems and an interesting plan he has for using the Waterway.

"Now traffic on the Waterway is largely limited to people moving great distances," he pointed out. "But it's much more manageable and practicable to enjoy the Waterway over shorter distances. Why not take people down interesting sections of it in houseboats, in convoy, rather like a covered wagon train? Have cassettes aboard that they can turn on at certain channel markers and hear about what they are seeing and its history. Have them go ashore at various places for lectures about the ecology, field trips, cookouts. That could develop into a whole new activity."

One afternoon I happened to be in the dockmaster's office at Harbour Town when an agitated man entered and asked for the sheriff's telephone number, saying, "Someone just shot at my boat." He offered no explanation, but since he made his call from a wall telephone I overheard his story.

In Calibogue Sound, he reported, his 60-foot cabin cruiser had passed a "wild-looking man" in a small sailboat, and the fellow had brandished a gun and *(Continued on page 166)*

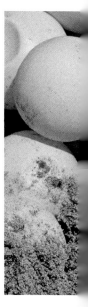

Trees destroyed by beach erosion mar part of the Atlantic edge of Daufuskie Island. Farther south, on Blackbeard Island, a seagoing loggerhead turtle lays its eggs at night under the eye of wildlife refuge official Ron Hight. The eggs, which look like table-tennis balls, number more than a hundred. Although the mother covers them with sand, marauding raccoons often find and eat them.

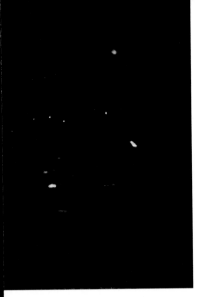

Coastal marshlands from South Carolina
to Florida support a variety of wildlife.
The alligator, largest predator of the
marshes, feeds on birds, fish, turtles,
raccoons, and other small animals.
Below, opposite, a white European
fallow deer stands alert on Little St.
Simons Island, Georgia. Sportsmen hunt
the deer during a limited fall season.
On Blackbeard Island, a snowy egret
spreads white wings. Once nearly anni-
hilated by plume hunters, egrets have
gradually increased under Federal protection and now commonly appear along
the southern part of the Waterway.

had then shot at the powerboat twice. Fortunately, no one had been hurt.

"Did he hit your boat?" I asked.

"I can't find any holes," he said.

Could the gunman have been Smiling Sam, the tattooed tough I saw at Bucksport? I never did find out. But if it was Sam, I'm sure he shot above the cruiser as a warning. He didn't look like a fellow who could miss a 60-foot boat.

At Hilton Head the Johnsons reluctantly left the warm southern autumn for the journey back to Princeton, but we linked up with two Annapolis friends, John Gardner, delivering a sailboat to Florida, and Susan McQueen. When we left the island for Thunderbolt, Georgia, John and Susan sailed aboard the 43-foot *Williwaw* in company with *Andromeda*.

*T*hunderbolt, a short run from Hilton Head, is a suburb of Savannah. Like Charleston, Savannah boasts magnificent restored homes, many on the parklike squares laid out by founder James Oglethorpe. Moreover, it can claim one of the South's most celebrated haunted houses.

When I called at the house it looked ordinary enough: a four-story, late 18th-century home with wooden superstructure and a brick foundation. Built in 1796, it was moved in 1963 from its original location on Bryan Street to 507 East St. Julian. Perhaps that's what stirred up the ghosts. Strange, loud noises and tools that moved about terrorized workmen. The owner heard footsteps and loud crashing noises; several guests heard a woman screaming; others saw a spectral gray-haired man in a gray suit.

Betty Lee and her physician husband, Lawrence, now own and live in the house. She showed me through the beautiful interior and described recent ghostly activity.

"Our son, sleeping in his bed on the top floor, had a heavy flower pot crash down on his head, cutting him. My husband, alone in the house, heard voices coming from the hi-fi—when it wasn't turned on. Another day he took a call from a patient on the kitchen telephone, then made an outside call; a few minutes later he went upstairs and found the telephone off the hook and on the bed. He could not have received or made a call if the phone had been like that several minutes earlier. Yet, again, he was alone in the house."

Mrs. Lee, an attractive matron not given to flights of fancy, told me of these events with a trace of amusement in her voice. She herself has heard footsteps and other sounds, but is not frightened. The ghosts of 507 East St. Julian Street, if ghosts there be, will have to share the premises, like it or not.

I returned to *Andromeda* in a fitful wind and rain that enveloped Thunderbolt for 48 hours. But when we left, following *Williwaw*, the day again turned golden. Such weather invites anchoring out, and we had arranged a rendezvous at Cow Pen Creek, deep in that sea of tawny marsh grass. Our route took us through a maze as intricate as the Waccamaw but open and spacious, with the endless grass radiant in the sun.

John and Susan pulled into narrow Cow Pen Creek, just off the Waterway, before we did and dropped anchor. Soon we came alongside, *Andromeda*'s stern to *Williwaw*'s bow, and put out our own anchor. That way the rafted boats would avoid swinging when the powerful flood tide sought out each stream and rivulet.

In this tranquil setting our two crews enjoyed a leisurely dinner in *Andromeda*'s cockpit, while watching evening shadows dull the gold that surrounded us. The first stars came out, and soon all the fires of heaven burned brilliantly, among them my beautiful constellation Andromeda. For a long while after the others retired, I communed with the celestial lady and her companions. Only humming insects and the nervous cackle of a marsh hen, disturbed by some nocturnal marauder, marred the deep quiet.

The morning dawned clear but chill, and all around us wraiths of vapor rose like smoke from pockets of warm sea water left by the flood tide. Both anchors had dragged, but not far, and soon the two boats again were under way.

We passed Blackbeard Island, a national wildlife refuge, and Sapelo Island, a refuge owned by the State of Georgia. Across Altamaha Sound and on down the Mackay River we cruised, finally tying up at a marina below the causeway bridge that links the mainland near Brunswick, Georgia, to St. Simons, one of the Golden Isles that is developed and easy of access.

Our marina occupied a niche on little Lanier Island, named for the Georgia poet Sidney Lanier, and just to the south at the mouth of the Brunswick River lay the Marshes of Glynn, immortalized in one of his best-known poems. Perhaps the sweep and spaciousness of the marsh are best captured in these lines:

> And what if behind me to westward
>   the wall of the woods stands high?
> The world lies east: how ample,
>   the marsh and the sea and the sky!
> A league and a league of marsh-grass,
>   waist-high, broad in the blade,
> Green, and all of a height,
>   and unflecked with a light or a shade,
> Stretch leisurely off, in a pleasant plain,
> To the terminal blue of the main.

The sea isles that Lanier knew more than a century ago have a history dating from 1521, when the Spanish discovered them. In 1526 Spaniards established the first European settlement in what is now the United States, near North Island, South Carolina, and later they spread to the Georgia islands. But these settlements did not survive, nor did a foothold established by the French on South Carolina's Parris Island in 1562.

On St. Simons we examined the ruins of Fort Frederica, a

Early-morning riders coax their horses into the Atlantic surf on Sea Island, Georgia.

THOMAS NEBBIA

surprisingly small stronghold considering the critically important role it played in colonial history. James Oglethorpe, Georgia's founder, directed its construction in 1736. Six years later the Spanish in Cuba and Florida, intent on wiping out all British settlers, sent 50 ships and 3,000 troops against Frederica. Oglethorpe and his 900 defenders turned back the invaders, who never again challenged British possession.

Change has touched very lightly such inhabited islands as Daufuskie and Johns in South Carolina waters, Sapelo and others in Georgia. They are not easy to reach, and the education and health care of their people, mostly black, have been problems for years. Dr. James Q. Gant, Jr., a physician now practicing in Washington, D. C., recalls with some amusement and with compassion his public health work on the Georgia isles in 1938. He was sent there by the Federal Government to launch a campaign against syphilis, hookworm, pellagra, and malaria.

"We made Brunswick our headquarters, and sent mobile clinics all over the area, trying to get people to come to us for blood tests for syphilis," Dr. Gant recalls. "Hardly anyone responded, despite posters everywhere offering syphilis tests. Finally a man said to me, 'Doctor, the word here for what you want to treat isn't syphilis. Call it bad blood.' So I did, and it worked. People came."

One isle the health teams never set foot on was ultra-exclusive Jekyll Island, then the site of a club where Rockefellers, Goulds, Vanderbilts, and Morgans spent the months between Christmas and Easter. Members, limited to 100, owned the island and closed it to everyone except invited guests. They built family "cottages" reminiscent of the mansions of Newport. This elite group, which reputedly controlled one-sixth of the world's wealth, gathered annually under the southern sun from 1886 until World War II forced abandonment of the retreat.

Today Jekyll Island is owned by the State of Georgia, and a bridge links it to the mainland south of Brunswick. We visited it by car and found motels, golf courses, a convention center, cocktail lounges, and shopping centers.

When *Andromeda* left Lanier Island for Fernandina Beach, Florida, our route wound through the marshes behind Cumberland Island, last and largest of Georgia's sea isles. Thomas Carnegie, brother of Andrew, bought most of that remote hideaway in the last century, and his descendants still live there. The National Park Foundation owns about a third of the island and would like to establish a national seashore where Cumberland's sands take the blows of the Atlantic.

But as yet no bridge links Cumberland to the mainland, so it has not suffered Jekyll's fate of commercialization and traffic. I pray it never will. Much of the charm of those golden marshes and of the Golden Isles themselves is their seclusion. Lose that, and for me much of the luster would be gone from the gold.

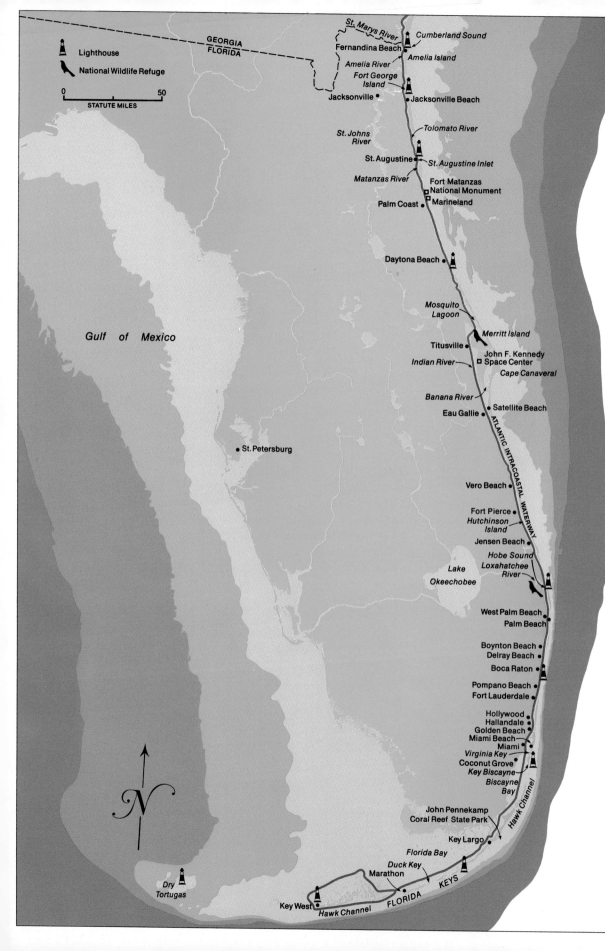

GEORGIA
FLORIDA

🗼 Lighthouse

🐦 National Wildlife Refuge

0   50
STATUTE MILES

St. Marys River
Cumberland Sound
Fernandina Beach
Amelia Island
Amelia River
Fort George Island
Jacksonville
Jacksonville Beach

Tolomato River
St. Johns River
St. Augustine
St. Augustine Inlet
Matanzas River
Fort Matanzas National Monument
Marineland
Palm Coast

Daytona Beach

Mosquito Lagoon
Merritt Island
Titusville
John F. Kennedy Space Center
Indian River
Cape Canaveral

Banana River
Satellite Beach
Eau Gallie

Gulf of Mexico

St. Petersburg

Vero Beach

Fort Pierce
Hutchinson Island

Jensen Beach

Hobe Sound
Loxahatchee River

Lake Okeechobee

West Palm Beach
Palm Beach

Boynton Beach
Delray Beach
Boca Raton

Pompano Beach
Fort Lauderdale

Hollywood
Hallandale
Golden Beach
Miami Beach
Miami
Virginia Key
Coconut Grove
Key Biscayne
Biscayne Bay

ATLANTIC INTRACOASTAL WATERWAY

John Pennekamp Coral Reef State Park

Hawk Channel

Key Largo

N

Florida Bay

Duck Key
Marathon

Dry Tortugas

FLORIDA KEYS

Key West   Hawk Channel

7

Florida: Cruising to the Winter Sun

*I*n the middle of Cumberland Sound, *Andromeda* sailed from Georgia into Florida over a boundary marked only by a gathering of raucous gulls. Minutes later, in the Amelia River, we passed Mile 715, indicated on our chart by a magenta line. It told us how far we had voyaged from Norfolk, a very distant and different world. Just ahead, off our port bow, lay the busy Fernandina Beach waterfront; beyond it the Intracoastal Waterway winds another 373 miles to Miami through a succession of glittering cities by the sea.

We found nothing glittering or resortlike, however, about workaday Fernandina. Two big, malodorous paper mills are the principal employers, but the town is also a shrimping center, and we powered past trawlers rafted together three deep at packing plants and along the waterfront's high bulkhead.

Old-timers claim Fernandina Beach started the commercial shrimp industry in the United States more than half a century ago, and each year in May residents commemorate that beginning with shrimp-boat races off the town docks. Imagine ponderous Clydesdale draft horses racing down a congested main street, and you'll have some idea of what those workboat contests are like: beamy, heavy trawlers vying for position with wide-open throttles!

Beyond the shrimp boats we drew abeam of the Florida Marine Welcome Station, a multicolored tepee of steel, concrete, and glass. Florida stocks the curious edifice with pretty girls and free orange juice, but we passed these attractions by and maneuvered *Andromeda*'s bulk into the little municipal yacht basin adjoining the center.

There we enjoyed our first mail call in nearly two weeks. We had arranged to have our mail sent to chambers of commerce along our route, and in Fernandina Beach a woman met us with letters as we tied up.

Following Florida's eastern seaboard, the Intracoastal route threads past historic St. Augustine and the Gold Coast cities from Vero Beach to Miami Beach, then heads southwest to the keys.

For three centuries Amelia Island, the site of Fernandina Beach, was one of the most coveted pieces of land in North America. The flags of six nations have flown over it: France, Spain, Great Britain, Mexico, the Confederacy, and the United States. In addition, some Amelia adventurers called the Patriots, who wanted union with the United States, briefly raised their own flag there early in the 19th century, and so did some mercenaries flying a banner called the Green Cross of Florida. Piracy, slave trading, smuggling, blockade running—Amelia Island saw them all.

A glance at the map shows what all the fuss was about: Fernandina was the nearest foreign port to the English colonies and later to the young, brawling United States, which did not acquire Florida until 1821. In the old days, as now, Cumberland Sound gave easy access to the Atlantic.

Little Fernandina is still a deepwater port of call with its own veteran harbor pilot, Capt. George T. Davis.

"I handle 130 to 140 ships each year," he told me. "I haven't missed one in 32 years. Now I'm the only pilot here, but back in the port's heyday around World War I, we had 13. Most of the freighters that put in here these days are foreign-owned, and they load pulpwood."

Captain Davis's great-grandfather, grandfather, father, two great-uncles, and an uncle all were harbor pilots in southern ports. Indeed, piloting traditionally has been a closely held family affair. All applicants nevertheless must undergo long apprenticeships and pass rigid written and oral examinations.

Davis recalls the story of a young candidate being examined by the pilot commissioners. They handed him a harbor chart and said:

"Now show us where the snags and rocks and shoals are."

"I don't know," responded the youngster.

"You mean you're applying for a pilot's license," one of the examiners sputtered, "and you don't know where the snags and rocks and shoals are?"

"I don't know where they're at, sir," the youth replied, "but I sure know where they ain't!"

Knowing where they ain't, said Captain Davis, is the secret of his own long, unmarred success in Cumberland Sound and the Amelia and St. Marys Rivers.

Amelia Island, though in Florida waters, is really the southernmost of the barrier Sea Islands that begin off South Carolina. Charles Fraser has purchased most of the southern end of Amelia and is constructing there an oceanfront community patterned after the one he built so successfully at Hilton Head.

Not far south of Amelia lies Fort George Island, a place with an evil, fascinating history. Zephaniah Kingsley, born in Scotland but reared in Charleston, moved to the island in 1813 and built what is now the oldest plantation house in Florida. On his

"Sheer enjoyment of sunshine, fresh air, wind, water, and speed" brings Becky Houchen of Miami to Biscayne Bay for an afternoon on her 16-foot Hobie Cat catamaran. The Ohio-bred schoolteacher took up sailing as a student at the University of Miami, and now races regularly.

Greedy for scraps, gulls pursue shrimp boats off Fernandina Beach, home port of an active shrimping

fleet since the turn of the century. Trawling from dawn to dark, a lucky boat will net 250 to 500 pounds.

island fief he trained thousands of slaves as skilled artisans, then sold them at premium prices.

I went by car to Kingsley's home, a big wood house with foundations of the region's traditional "tabby," a mixture of oyster shell, sand, and lime. The State of Florida now owns the place. Despite sunny weather and a pleasant woman curator, Kingsley Plantation depressed me; the strange, paradoxical personality of its onetime master, wicked yet benign, ruthless yet compassionate, seemed to permeate the atmosphere.

Zephaniah Kingsley bought and sold blacks, yet he married the daughter of an African chief. He put himself above the law, yet he fought bravely for the civil rights denied freedmen in the South. He wrote a treatise defending slavery, yet he established a colony of freedmen in Haiti. He thought blacks destined for bondage, yet he proclaimed them the mental equals and physical superiors of whites. He treated slaves with kindness, permitting dancing, merrymaking, and even private farming for profit; yet I saw the hot, windowless cell where slaves who displeased him spent weeks in solitary confinement.

"The best we can do in this world is to balance evils judiciously," Kingsley once said in an attempt to explain himself. A vain man, arrogating to himself godlike judgment; a twisted, willful man, preaching humanity yet profiting from the misery of countless people.

*T*he weather next morning, though intermittently sunny, had turned quite chill, and Mike and I were back in the thermal underwear we wore during the windy cold snap at Bucksport. We cruised for several miles through water sudsy and dirty-looking with the effluent from one of the paper mills. Then, beyond Jacksonville Beach, our route took us through dense growth marred by the shattered, forlorn trunks of many palm trees, presumably storm victims. But we enjoyed the wide Tolomato River, little developed and pleasant to the eye all the way to St. Augustine, where we tied up at the city dock.

Mike and I liked St. Augustine despite itself. The nation's oldest city is unrestrained in its pitch for tourists, hawking such attractions as the Fountain of Youth, the Old Jail, the Oldest House, the Oldest Wooden School, and a host of other buildings. Actually, few authentic old structures have survived the numerous pillages of the place, but the Historic St. Augustine Preservation Board has restored several venerable shops and homes and has reconstructed others with painstaking accuracy. The Spanish kept such detailed records that architects and builders have been able to resurrect a considerable part of the colonial town. We strolled about, watching leatherworker, blacksmith, weaver, and other craftsmen, fancying we were Spanish settlers in town for market day.

Castillo de San Marcos, the massive waterfront fort, commands St. Augustine Inlet and the Matanzas River. Few communities

Massive Castillo de San Marcos broods over the Intracoastal Waterway at St. Augustine, the nation's oldest European settlement, founded in 1565. Walls of coquina limestone, 13 feet thick at the base, withstood the British siege of 1702 that reduced the rest of the city to rubble. Cannon line the battlements (far right). Bearing the flag of Spain, Earl Manucy leads the Easter Festival Parade honoring the royal court of 1672, the year construction of the Castillo began.

can boast a more dramatic focal point or impressive showplace.

Spaniards founded St. Augustine in 1565, more than 40 years before the first permanent English settlement in Virginia, but they did not begin construction of this fort until 1672. Mindful that their town had once been burned to the ground, they built the Castillo as if for eternity, quarrying stone and fitting the massive blocks into thick walls and high battlements. The fort withstood several British attacks, although the town was burned one more time.

Today Castillo de San Marcos is a carefully preserved national monument, and each year more than half a million visitors climb its parapets and walk its well-kept paths and lawns.

Two of the 21,000 people moving to Florida each month listen to a real estate agent describing the new planned community of Palm Coast (opposite), under construction between St. Augustine and Daytona Beach. The Waterway borders the development (top); model homes, a welcome center, and a golf course lie beyond houses built along the canals.

When *Andromeda* resumed her southbound voyage, the winding Matanzas took us through some marshy areas, and there we observed a strange phenomenon. Off to starboard thousands and thousands of birds blackened a portion of the sky. Circling and dipping, now clustering, now scattering, they flew in a vast flock — perhaps I should say swarm. There was a strange unison in their swirling patterns, their abrupt soaring and quick descents. Here was the mad ballet of moths round a flame, the massed sweep and dip of migrating locusts.

As we neared the scene we could see the birds were small and gray, and we presumed them to be chimney swifts. Experts later supported the identification, and said such flocking during autumnal migration was common. But we had never witnessed such dervish aerobatics; they seemed to express an exuberant abandon, a wild ecstasy unknown to other creatures. Yet we could rejoice with the birds in the height of their sky and the wideness of their world.

Soon we passed Rattlesnake Island where the grim pile of Fort Matanzas, a small, Spanish-built outpost of Castillo de San Marcos, stood gray against the sky. Near the island in 1565 Don Pedro Menéndez de Avilés, the founder of St. Augustine, captured a large group of French Huguenots shipwrecked on the coast. Menéndez ordered their hands tied, and then the Frenchmen were led in groups of ten behind sand dunes where the soldiers stabbed them to death. Nearly 300 men were slaughtered; indeed, *matanzas* means "slaughters."

Marineland of Florida, pioneers in the training of porpoises and pilot whales for water shows, adjoins the Waterway only a few miles south of Matanzas Inlet, and we put in to its modern

Surfboards and jalopies, Frisbees and motor-
bikes — or simply sunshine — keep more than
200,000 college students happy during their
spring migration to the Daytona Beach
resort area from campuses across the
country. Their cars and campers (above)
crowd the central section of a 23-mile
stretch of hard-packed white sand, scene of
record-setting automobile races before the
Daytona International Speedway opened in
1959. No-nonsense police, hundreds of motels,
and the area's 100,000 residents brace for
the month-long invasion, an annual custom
that began in Fort Lauderdale in the early
1950's, then spread to other Florida beaches.

marina to see the last show of the day and to spend the night.

Next morning our route south followed a land cut, and we passed right through Palm Coast, the most ambitious real estate development in Florida. ITT Community Development Corporation has purchased about 100,000 acres, including some five miles of uninhabited beach on the Atlantic and more than 17 miles of land along the Intracoastal Waterway. Here the company is building a community it expects to grow to 650,000 people by the year 2000.

From a small dock on the Waterway, prospective buyers arriving by car were ferried by paddle-wheel boat up a canal to Palm Coast's model-homes area. No other home-sites had then been carved from the spartina grass and saltbushes, but the project has developed rapidly since our visit.

At Daytona Beach we passed through four drawbridges in quick succession, then spun the wheel to starboard and took the well-marked channel into the municipal yacht basin. Again we found Gene Hebert and his family docked near us aboard *Nevermore*, and they reported a leisurely passage, with numerous stops.

At Daytona Beach I met the old man Mike and I later referred to as Barnacle Bill. About 70 and skinny as a heron, he wore dirty sneakers, faded blue jeans held up by a rope, an old pea jacket, and a knitted cap pulled rakishly over his right ear. Hair sprouted from his left ear like a misplaced eyebrow. A stubble of gray beard covered his cheeks, and his seamed face contracted and expanded vigorously as he chewed a huge wad of tobacco.

"Saw you bring your boat in here," he said in a raspy voice. "She's a beauty."

"Thanks. We like her."

"Mine's that blue sloop over there," he added, gesturing toward a little wooden boat with a raked mast. "I'd like to take off again, but I don't have any crew."

"Why don't you advertise in a boating magazine for a girl or two to go with you?" I suggested.

I immediately regretted my facetious remark. The man was not only a complete stranger but a most unlikely-looking candidate for romance. Still, the kind of ad I proposed was not uncommon in boating magazines.

Far from being offended, the old man replied with a nod of agreement and a deft bit of one-upmanship: "I did advertise—

Apollo 16 soars moonward from Kennedy Space Center as spectators watch from boats seven miles away on the Banana River. At the Center, Merritt Island National Wildlife Refuge shelters some 250 bird species, including the common egret (opposite).

Morning sunlight touches sabal palms and cypress—some killed by salt water—on the mangrove-lined

Loxahatchee River. Florida's Waterway route crosses the river, haunt of alligators and manatees.

and got five applications. Then something came up and I couldn't make the cruise. But I've kept in touch with one of those women. She said, 'Whenever you're ready to go, I'm ready.' I think I'll call her tonight."

We rented a car at Daytona Beach primarily for the experience of driving on the city's famous expanse of hard-packed sand adjoining the Atlantic surf. There, for six decades, many automobile and motorcycle speed records were set. Florida classified the beach as a highway, and cars are still permitted on part of it, though strictly for fun and at low speed. We drove just inside the surf, keeping a wary eye out for strollers.

One elderly man carried a metal disk on a rod, and he passed it slowly over the surface of the beach. I recognized it as a metal detector. Scanning for Spanish doubloons washed up from the sea! I stopped and introduced myself to Ray Brodbeck, a retired electrical contractor from Peoria, Illinois.

"No treasure around here," he said, laughing. "Occasionally you find a Spanish coin around Vero Beach or Fort Pierce, but it's rare. I just look for lost coins; last year I found 2,422, plus 18 rings. It's a hobby."

He buried a coin in the sand and let me listen to the buzzing sound in his earphones as the detector passed above it. Fascinated, I watched Mr. Brodbeck scan a large area; finally he discovered something that evoked a clamor from his machine. Two elderly ladies also had been watching, and now, quite excited, they asked if they could dig it up.

"You do that, ladies, and I'll give you half of whatever you find," said Mr. Brodbeck. He was even more generous when they unearthed their prize: an old hubcap—just what he had expected. While we laughed at the expressions on their faces, he gave them title to the whole thing, and the pair of good sports bore it away as a souvenir.

When *Andromeda* resumed her cruise she carried two additional crewmen: Ken Grine, a retired Air Force lieutenant colonel, and his wife, Bobbie, from Satellite Beach, Florida. Ken had taken me in tow when I was a young aviation writer, beginning a friendship that has endured more than 20 years.

Again the weather had turned cold, and all of us wore such heavy clothing we looked more like guests at a ski lodge than sailors. But no one minded; it was the eve of Thanksgiving, the chill seemed appropriate, and we were bound for the Grines' home and the traditional turkey.

Our destination, Eau Gallie, lay 98 miles from Daytona Beach, a long day's run for a sailboat. In the broad waters of Mosquito Lagoon we opened up the throttle of *Andromeda*'s engine.

Pelicans crossed our bow or soared beside us, their flight as effortless as that of thistledown. Cormorants assembled in grave groups atop the navigational markers. No other species joined them, and we decided they were either avian pariahs or did not like to share their perches.

Traversing Haulover Canal, we passed from Mosquito Lagoon into the broad upper reaches of the Indian River, where the west wind got a long fetch at us. I gladly surrendered the cold metal wheel to Ken and scanned the Merritt Island shore off to port. Below Titusville I found what I sought: the distant but obviously huge Vehicle Assembly Building at NASA's Kennedy Space Center. This structure, one of the largest in the world, housed the towering Apollo moon rockets before they were moved to their launch pads.

With that building abeam, we were at about the spot where Mike and I had witnessed the lift-off of Apollo 16 the previous spring. Then we were aboard *Sea Hunter*, an oceanographic research vessel of the Florida Institute of Technology. The weather that day was fair though hazy, and at the moment of firing a burst of flame eclipsed the rocket, which we could barely see on the horizon. Slowly, as if reluctant to leave Mother Earth, Apollo 16 cleared the flame and then rose atop a long streamer of fire, accelerating rapidly. At high altitude the rocket plumed a contrail, and then it was lost to view.

I had watched a score of military rockets fired from Cape Canaveral before there was a NASA or a plan to put men on the moon. In those days we had viewed the shots from roadblocks uncomfortably close to the firing pads. On one occasion I dived under a truck when an Atlas missile blew up in midair and showered burning debris.

Yet the launching of Apollo 16, even though disappointingly distant from our vantage point, gave me a greater thrill. Three men rode the Apollo; incredibly, they were on their way to another world. When I began writing about aviation, few aeronautical engineers would discuss space travel lest they be thought impractical dreamers. How fast we had progressed to Apollo 16 in that long journey that one day will take mankind out among the stars!

We continued on down the Indian River at nearly full throttle, knowing we must reach the bridge at Eau Gallie before 4:15 p.m., when it would be closed to boats so that it could handle rush-hour auto traffic. With barely five minutes to spare *Andromeda* passed through the bridge, and we turned into Eau Gallie's protected harbor.

Eau Gallie was our first rest stop since Hilton Head, and we spent several days sight-seeing and enjoying the hospitality of the Grines at their nearby home.

On Thanksgiving Day *Nevermore* pulled into the marina with a fuel leak. Gene Hebert cured it, but we resumed our journey before he and his family were ready to leave, and as it turned out that was the last we saw of them. Deirdre, the oldest child, seemed to anticipate that it would be our last encounter; she asked to take a picture to remember us by.

During our voyage we had found that the marine weather

NATHAN BENN (BELOW)

Rising in his stirrups, a home-team player moves in on the ball during a match with Milwaukee at the Royal Palm Polo Grounds in Boca Raton, "winter polo capital of the world." Farther north on the Gold Coast chain of expensive resorts, Palm Beach retains its old elegance and exclusiveness from the turn of the century, when railroad magnate Henry M. Flagler established it as the winter home of America's plutocracy— the Newport of the South. Fashionable shops line Worth Avenue (opposite), where David's Palm Beach displays fine costume jewelry of coral, enamel, and spinel; a chauffeur waits patiently outside. Helene Newman, co-owner of the Lullabye Shop, chats with Mrs. William R. O'Connor of Connecticut and Palm Beach, who drives her own restored 1934 Bentley Open Tourer. Says Mrs. O'Connor, a winter resident for 45 years, "I am very greatly afflicted with the rare disease of old-car-itis."

Glow of gold leaf suffuses the living room of Mar-A-Lago, Marjorie Merriweather Post's Palm Beach estate. Chandeliers of Bristol glass hang from a copy of the Thousand-Winged Ceiling of the Venetian Academy; silk-needlework panels adorn walls pierced by Moorish archways. A photograph of the famed businesswoman and philanthropist, taken a few years after the mansion's completion in 1927, rests on an inlaid table (left). Upon Mrs. Post's death in 1973 at the age of 86, Mar-A-Lago passed to the Federal Government, to serve as a guesthouse for foreign dignitaries.

NATHAN BENN (BELOW)

forecasts, particularly wind predictions, sometimes bore small resemblance to what we actually experienced. Our log records just such an extreme variance on the day we left Eau Gallie for Vero Beach:

"Got under way at 1015 hours. Small-craft warnings had been lifted, and the prediction was for decreasing winds and improving conditions. But the weather—overcast, chill, and showery —became filthier with each passing minute and each mile. Blowing at least 20 knots out of the west when we pulled into Riomar Bay Yacht Club, and getting colder. Found the club had put back up its small-craft warning flag. We have not had a warm, sunny day since entering Florida."

So back into thermal underwear that day, absurd as it seemed when more than halfway down Florida's east coast. The temperature tumbled to 40° at night, and the wind blew gustily for two days. But we enjoyed the handsome community of Vero Beach. From there south, Florida takes on its "Gold Coast" look of opulence.

*D*espite the cold, we were on the verge of entering that part of Florida warmed by proximity to the Gulf Stream. South of Jensen Beach tropical flora makes an appearance, and the air softens. By the time the Waterway reaches Palm Beach, where the Gulf Stream is only a mile or so offshore, Florida is summery except during brief incursions of arctic air.

We left Vero Beach in cloudy weather, with a warming trend evident. Our dredged route took us through wide but shallow waters with disposal islands scattered about in green profusion. Driftwood shacks built by squatters could be seen on some of the islands, but pelicans seemed the *de facto* owners.

The weather yielded to the Gulf Stream, and it was summer again and clear when we docked at Jensen Beach. Here two old friends from the Chesapeake's Eastern Shore, El and Peg Watkins, became our guides. Until he retired to Florida, El had owned our favorite Chesapeake Bay marina, an immaculate place at Oxford.

On Hutchinson Island the Watkinses took us to the marine museum of the Martin County Historical Society at the House of Refuge, a gaunt old cypress-shingle building surrounded by big tanks where young turtles from a state hatchery nearby scrabbled and swam aimlessly. Most were green turtles; there were also some loggerheads and one hawksbill.

Each year from June through August, giant sea turtles crawl up on the beaches of Hutchinson Island to lay their eggs in the sand. People often disturb the nests, although it is against the law, and raccoons and other animals take a severe toll. So scientists and volunteers dig up eggs and take them to the hatchery, where about a thousand young turtles are born annually. They are kept in tanks a year before being released into the sea.

"Hawksbill turtles are hunted for their shells, loggerheads for

Intracoastal Waterway passes through Fort Lauderdale, the state's leading yacht center, where

gleaming pleasure boat ties up at almost every palm-shaded house on the community's many canals.

their eggs, and green turtles for their eggs and meat," said Richard Carr, a keeper at the House of Refuge. "Hunting them or stealing their eggs has endangered most species of sea turtle."

A diet of crab meat and fish obviously agreed with Captain Louie, a loggerhead that had lived in a cistern for all his 16 years. Richard said Captain Louie weighed 600 pounds.

The rugged old building's name comes from its original purpose: It was one of ten houses of refuge built by the Federal Government along Florida's east coast between St. Augustine and Biscayne Bay. A keeper and his family were stationed at each to provide help and shelter for shipwreck victims who managed to get ashore on the isolated coast, and to aid travelers on the Indian River.

Our passage from Jensen Beach to West Palm Beach took us through Hobe Sound, where to starboard we could see a wildlife refuge and to port a succession of mansions set among emerald lawns that sweep down to the shore. I've heard it said that Hobe Sound is a refuge for people who find Palm Beach not exclusive enough. Still, the Palm Beach docks remain sufficiently exclusive — and so crowded with huge yachts — that we, like most transients, went directly to the municipal marina in West Palm Beach.

Henry M. Flagler literally put Palm Beach on the map. The area was a wilderness until opened up by his Florida East Coast Railway in the Gay Nineties, and there he built his gigantic Royal Poinciana, largest resort hotel in the world when it opened in 1894. It soon became the most fashionable in the nation. The structure was torn down years ago.

Today high-rises as well as mansions line the city's ocean and lake fronts. Invariably white or light-colored, they give Palm Beach a look of cleanliness fully warranted upon closer inspection by land. Flagler's huge stone Whitehall, on Lake Worth, still ranks among the most gleaming buildings in town. After his death in 1913 it became a hotel, but it has since been restored as a museum and looks much as it did when the old empire builder kept its 16 guest rooms filled.

Our friends Bob and Mary Elizabeth Shelton had flown down from Annapolis to join us for ten days, and were aboard as we motored leisurely from Palm Beach toward Fort Lauderdale. The attitude of all of us might best be described as one of awe. Luxury on a truly astounding scale surrounded us. Towering, beautifully landscaped condominiums interspersed with large homes, many with patios and swimming pools screened against insects; bordered not only the Waterway but also the myriad canals at

Year-round playground of Miami Beach boasts the world's densest array of luxury hotels, crowding all available space from oceanfront to boat-lined Collins Avenue. In 1972 the resort attracted three million vacationists, many lured by its night life. Opposite, dancers perform in a lavish revue at the Playboy Plaza.

right angles to it. Docks held yachts of a size that made *Andromeda* seem a dinghy by comparison.

Boynton Beach, Delray Beach, Boca Raton, Pompano Beach—one glittering community after another passed in review. Development was so closely packed we felt we were sight-seeing on a downtown street.

The Sheltons live on Crab Creek, neighbor of our own Church Creek, and like us are used to trees and fields and a woodland quiet. We could all be impressed by, but we could not envy, the lavishness of our surroundings.

We progressed to "the Venice of America." Fort Lauderdale has 270 miles of canals—compared to only 45 in Venice—and it is here that Gold Coast living attains its ultimate expression.

Views of the luxurious homes adjoining the waterfront can best be enjoyed from one of the sight-seeing boats that ply the waters. Rather than use our own boat, we relaxed and let the captain of a paddle-wheeler pick the route.

Two such excursion boats are based at famous Bahia Mar Yachting Center. Indeed, it seemed just about everything must be based there when we approached the fuel dock for a slip assignment. The marina is one of the world's largest, with hundreds of boats, a maze of docks, swimming pool, shopping center, post office, big motor hotel, and one of Fort Lauderdale's finest restaurants.

It's difficult to imagine a hanging at such a pleasant place, but it happened. The year was 1929, and a Coast Guard station occupied the site of Bahia Mar. James Alderman, a rumrunner, had killed two Coast Guardsmen and wounded a Secret Service agent in an offshore gun battle. He was sentenced to death at Fort Lauderdale, but local officials balked at carrying out the sentence. A Federal judge, acting under an old law, ordered Alderman's execution at the nearest Federal post—the Coast Guard station. There, in a seaplane hangar, the killer dropped from a gallows. For the only time in history, a man had been hanged at a U. S. Coast Guard installation.

While at Fort Lauderdale we left *Andromeda* to drive back to

Kennedy Space Center for the dramatic night launch of Apollo 17, last of the series carrying Americans to the moon. This time we viewed the shot from the press stands, in dramatic proximity to exhaust flames that lit up the night like noonday and shattered the air with an intensity of noise that could be felt as a pulsing resonance in our chest cavities. No one who experienced Apollo 17, I felt, could doubt mankind's destiny among the stars.

Our return to Fort Lauderdale brought the melancholy realization that *Andromeda*'s long voyage down the Atlantic Coast's water highway was about to end. Boating had become a zestful and healthy way of life for Mike and Bill and me, but now only one brief voyage of 24 miles, from Bahia Mar to Coconut Grove just south of Miami, lay ahead of us. We put the Sheltons on a plane for home and got *Andromeda* shipshape for the last leg of her passage to the sun.

But a study of the Waterway chart revealed a complication. I counted 12 drawbridges between Bahia Mar and Coconut Grove, and nearly all would have hours when they were closed to boat traffic. Getting *Andromeda* and her tall mast down that crowded stretch of Waterway looked like the biggest tussle of the entire trip. So I decided to go outside in the ocean.

That left one problem: how to see the stretch of the Waterway I would miss if we took the ocean route. John Yeager, the young manager of Bahia Mar's boating facilities, offered to take me to Miami in *Red Snapper*, the barn-red, 22-foot powerboat owned by *Motor Boating & Sailing Magazine*.

Not far from Bahia Mar we passed through Port Everglades, deepest harbor in Florida. It's also the biggest cruise port in the South, a busy commercial basin, and a surprising contrast to the resort atmosphere of Fort Lauderdale and Hollywood, the two communities in which it lies. No shiny cruise ships lay at the docks that day, but several big vessels were unloading petroleum and building materials.

For a time after Port Everglades the rather narrow Waterway passed through an ugly commercial area, but at Hollywood Beach the expensive condominiums resumed, and at Hallandale tremendous high-rises literally walled us in, many with balconies where elderly people gravely watched our progress.

Lapped by emerald shoal waters half a mile off Key Biscayne, a weekend cottage rises 15 feet on concrete pilings at Stiltsville, a flotilla of some 15 houses—or less, depending on the severity of the most recent hurricane. Opposite, new arrivals join other holiday guests at the waterbound retreat, owned by a Coconut Grove marina. Sand-weighted chessmen await players on a shag-rug board.

Golden Beach relieved the sense of canyonlike enclosure with a number of elegant single-family dwellings, but again I felt we traveled a city street.

It was a relief to emerge from all that masonry into the open waters of Biscayne Bay. The sun shone brilliantly, and a brisk head wind showered us pleasantly with occasional rainbows of spray as John took us down the bay to Miamarina, the City of Miami's new, ultramodern boat refuge next to Bayfront Park in the heart of the downtown district.

The Plummers—of *The Boy, Me and the Cat*—upon attaining their journey's end in March 1913, tied up in the Miami River not far from the present site of Bayfront Park. They found the city hot, crude, and depressing, a stark contrast to modern Miami. On the day before they left for the north, Henry Plummer made a sad entry in his log about Scotty, the cat:

"On returning alone to the boat one night . . . Scotty failed to meet me at the rail. To my call I soon heard her little feet scrabbling across decks and before I could catch her in my arms she fell into the cockpit and with a little paw on my foot, died. . . . The heat, the noise, the smell, too much for little Scotty. You who love animals will know how we missed that little bunch of fur, and you who don't are of little account anyway. We gave her a sailor's burial in the Miami River and by mutual understanding have not mentioned her name since."

Marvels of marine life delight Patti Hurley of Stone Mountain, Georgia, just up from a dive off Key Largo at John Pennekamp Coral Reef State Park. Opposite, blue striped grunts and porkfish with black-striped faces mill near Key Largo Dry Rocks.

On the way back to Bahia Mar, John pulled into a marina for fuel. Across the Waterway bulldozers leveled a very extensive area, and dredges sucked silt from the water and dumped it behind new bulkheads.

"What's going in there?" I asked the marina manager.

"Oh, they're building 20,000 apartments," he said. I asked whether he meant 2,000, but he repeated his statement as matter-of-factly as if he were telling me the time.

Next day, with the clear, breezy weather holding, we took *Andromeda* out the inlet at Port Everglades, passing through a phalanx of high-rises to the ocean's edge, and then set the sails and turned the bow almost due south. *Andromeda* responded with unusual eagerness as we trimmed the sheets for a reach. She was free of enclosure and enjoying a day of blue water and blue skies. Off to starboard the white towers rose, but we stayed well offshore, glorying in this last sail.

We held our course past Miami Beach, past Virginia Key and Key Biscayne. I was sorely tempted to continue on down Hawk Channel into the long arc of the Florida Keys, retracing the route we had brought *Andromeda* the previous spring. The plush development so characteristic of the southern Florida mainland is well under way now in these islands, notably with such new, water-oriented resorts as those at Key Largo and Duck Key. American sun-seekers who once headed for retreats in the Bahamas and elsewhere in the West Indies are turning increasingly to tropic isles of their own.

Hawk Channel lies on the Atlantic side of the keys; the shallow Intracoastal runs down Florida Bay behind the protective barrier of the islands. Near Marathon, midpoint of the chain, boats take either the Gulf of Mexico or Hawk Channel to romantic old Key West, once a pirate haven. After commissioning our new *Andromeda* in St. Petersburg, we had made Marathon a port of call, and I vowed then that one day we would sail all the way to Key West—and perhaps beyond to the Dry Tortugas, the tiny isles some 70 miles farther west.

But for now, as much as we would have liked to follow a carefree course southward from Miami, Christmas was almost upon us, and strong ties of sentiment and family impelled us to fly north and home.

So we turned to starboard into the dogleg of Biscayne Channel, ran across Biscayne Bay, and then continued under power down narrow Dinner Key Channel to a marina at Coconut Grove. *Andromeda* would winter in southern Florida, and Bill Gay and some friends would bring her northward with the greening of the land.

Mike, Bill, and I shook hands rather solemnly, and the long voyage was over. After spending six months on *Andromeda* and traveling thousands of miles, we could say—and mean it—"I'd like to do it again!"

*I*n Kenneth Grahame's classic, *The Wind in the Willows*, the Sea Rat hikes through the English countryside, intent on returning to the sea to steal aboard a ship, and he tries to persuade young Water Rat, who lives on a sylvan river, to follow him and begin a life at sea:

"Take the Adventure, heed the call, now ere the irrevocable moment passes! 'Tis but a banging of the door behind you, a blithesome step forward, and you are out of the old life and into the new! . . . I will linger, and look back; and at last I will surely see you coming, eager and light-hearted, with all the South in your face!"

Alas, Water Rat did not accept the invitation. But I hope you will accept mine. Set forth in our wake, and perhaps somewhere along the Intracoastal Waterway you will chance upon *Andromeda*. Together we will turn our faces toward the southern sun and sail on and on, rejoicing in our freedom.

Enthusiastic Key Wester by adoption, guide Elma Ketchum welcomes visitors to the Ernest Hemingway Home and recalls her husband's friendship with the writer: "They used to spend hours just sitting under a tree, talking." The famed author wrote most of his novels while living at Key West from 1928 to 1940. Joker, a descendant of some of the 50 cats Hemingway kept around the place, lounges on a chair.

EMORY KRISTOF, NATIONAL GEOGRAPHIC STAFF

Cayos—"little islands"—the Spanish called the crescent of Florida Keys, now linked by the Over

...eas Highway for more than 150 miles from Biscayne Bay to Key West, beyond the distant clouds.

Index

Boldface indicates illustrations; italic refers to picture captions.

Library of Congress ℗ Data

Fisher, Allan C., Jr.
  America's inland waterway
  1. Intracoastal Waterway. 2. Atlantic
coast—Description and travel.
3. Fisher, Allan C., Jr.
I. Title
F106.F49   917.5   73-831
ISBN 87044-128-0

Acknowledgments

The Special Publications Division is grateful to the people named or quoted in the text and to those listed here for their generous cooperation and assistance during the preparation of this book:

Capt. Irwin Jenkins, Chief Pilot, The Atlantic Coast Pilots; Thomas E. King, Executive Vice President, St. Augustine and St. Johns County (Fla.) Chamber of Commerce; Lynn H. Nicholas, Robert C. Nicholas III, and Richard B. Nye, nautical consultants; Robert H. Shields, Bureau of Sport Fisheries and Wildlife, U. S. Department of the Interior; Smithsonian Institution; Sidney J. Wain, Publisher and President, and the entire staff of *Waterway Guide,* Annapolis, Md.; U. S. Army Corps of Engineers: District Offices, North and South Atlantic Divisions, and Locke L. Mouton, Office of the Chief of Engineers, Washington, D. C.; U. S. Coast Guard: Third, Fifth, and Seventh Districts, and Capt. Terry McDonald, Special Assistant in the Office of Public Affairs, Headquarters, Washington, D. C.

Composition for *America's Inland Waterway* by National Geographic's Phototypographic Division, Carl M. Shrader, Chief; Lawrence F. Ludwig, Assistant Chief. Printed and bound by Fawcett Printing Corp., Rockville, Md. Color separation by Chanticleer Co., Inc., New York, N.Y.; Colorgraphics, Inc., Beltsville, Md.; Graphic Color Plate, Inc., Stamford, Conn.; Progressive Color Corp., Rockville, Md.; and J. Wm. Reed Co., Alexandria, Va.

NATIONAL GEOGRAPHIC SOCIETY

WASHINGTON, D. C.

Organized "for the increase and diffusion of geographic knowledge"

GILBERT HOVEY GROSVENOR

Editor, 1899-1954; President, 1920-1954
Chairman of the Board, 1954-1966

THE NATIONAL GEOGRAPHIC SOCIETY is chartered in Washington, D. C., in accordance with the laws of the United States, as a nonprofit scientific and educational organization for increasing and diffusing geographic knowledge and promoting research and exploration. Since 1890 the Society has supported 942 explorations and research projects, adding immeasurably to man's knowledge of earth, sea, and sky. It diffuses this knowledge through its monthly journal, NATIONAL GEOGRAPHIC; more than 30 million maps distributed each year; its books, globes, atlases, and filmstrips; 30 School Bulletins a year in color; information services to press, radio, and television; technical reports; exhibits from around the world in Explorers Hall; and a nationwide series of programs on television.

MELVIN M. PAYNE, President
ROBERT E. DOYLE, Vice President and Secretary
GILBERT M. GROSVENOR, Vice President
THOMAS M. BEERS, Vice President and Associate Secretary
HILLEARY F. HOSKINSON, Treasurer
OWEN R. ANDERSON, WILLIAM T. BELL,
LEONARD J. GRANT, W. EDWARD ROSCHER,
C. VERNON SANDERS, Associate Secretaries

BOARD OF TRUSTEES

MELVILLE BELL GROSVENOR
Chairman of the Board and Editor-in-Chief

THOMAS W. McKNEW, Advisory Chairman of the Board

LLOYD H. ELLIOTT, President,
George Washington University
CRAWFORD H. GREENEWALT
Chairman, Finance Committee,
E. I. du Pont de Nemours & Company
GILBERT M. GROSVENOR
Editor, National Geographic
ARTHUR B. HANSON, General
Counsel, National Geographic Society
CARYL P. HASKINS, Former
President, Carnegie Institution
of Washington
CARLISLE H. HUMELSINE
President, The Colonial Williamsburg
Foundation
CURTIS E. LeMAY, Former Chief
of Staff, U. S. Air Force
H. RANDOLPH MADDOX
Former Vice President, American
Telephone & Telegraph Company
WM. McCHESNEY MARTIN, JR.
Former Chairman, Board of
Governors, Federal Reserve System
BENJAMIN M. McKELWAY
Former Editor, Washington *Star*
MELVIN M. PAYNE, President,
National Geographic Society
LAURANCE S. ROCKEFELLER
President, Rockefeller Brothers Fund

ROBERT C. SEAMANS, JR.
President, National Academy
of Engineering
JUAN T. TRIPPE, Honorary
Chairman of the Board,
Pan American World Airways
FREDERICK G. VOSBURGH
Former Editor, National Geographic
JAMES H. WAKELIN, JR., Former
Assistant Secretary of Commerce
for Science and Technology
EARL WARREN, Former
Chief Justice of the United States
JAMES E. WEBB, Former
Administrator, National Aeronautics
and Space Administration
ALEXANDER WETMORE
Research Associate,
Smithsonian Institution
LLOYD B. WILSON (Emeritus)
Honorary Board Chairman,
Chesapeake & Potomac
Telephone Company
CONRAD L. WIRTH, Former
Director, National Park Service
LOUIS B. WRIGHT, Former
Director, Folger Shakespeare
Library

COMMITTEE FOR RESEARCH AND EXPLORATION

ALEXANDER WETMORE and MELVIN M. PAYNE, Vice Chairmen
EDWIN W. SNIDER, Secretary
BARRY C. BISHOP, National Geographic Staff, GILBERT M. GROSVENOR, MELVILLE BELL GROSVENOR, CARYL P. HASKINS, THOMAS W. McKNEW, ROBERT C. SEAMANS, JR., T. DALE STEWART, Physical Anthropologist Emeritus, Smithsonian Institution, MATTHEW W. STIRLING, Research Associate, Smithsonian Institution, JAMES H. WAKELIN, JR., FRANK C. WHITMORE, JR., Research Geologist, U. S. Geological Survey, CONRAD L. WIRTH, FREDERICK G. VOSBURGH, and PAUL A. ZAHL

Assistant Secretaries of the Society:
FRANK S. DELK, JOSEPH B. HOGAN,
RAYMOND T. McELLIGOTT, JR., EDWIN W. SNIDER
Assistant Treasurer: WARD S. PHELPS

Leonard J. Grant, Editorial Assistant to the President; Edwin W. Snider, Richard E. Pearson, Administrative Assistants to the President; Judith N. Dixon, Administrative Assistant to the Chairman and Editor-in-Chief; Lenore W. Kessler, Administrative Assistant to the Advisory Chairman of the Board

SECRETARY'S STAFF: *Administrative:* Earl Corliss, Jr., Harriet Carey, Frederick C. Gale. *Accounting:* Jay H. Givans, Alfred J. Hayre, William G. McGhee, Martha Allen Baggett. *Membership Promotion and Statistics:* Charles T. Kneeland (Chief), Thomas M. Kent. *Payroll and Retirement:* Howard R. Hudson (Supervisor); Mary L. Whitmore, Dorothy L. Dameron (Assistants). *Procurement:* J. P. M. Johnston, Thomas L. Fletcher, Robert G. Corey, Sheila H. Immel. *Membership Fulfillment:* Geneva S. Robinson, Paul B. Tylor, Peter F. Woods. *Computer Center:* Lewis P. Lowe. *Promotion:* Robert J. Warfel, Towne Windom, F. William Rath. *Printing:* Joe M. Barlett, Frank S. Oliverio. *Production Control:* James P. Kelly. *Personnel:* James B. Mahon, Adrian L. Loftin, Jr., Glenn G. Pepperman, Nellie E. Sinclair. *Medical:* Thomas L. Hartman, M.D. *Translation:* Zbigniew Jan Lutyk

NATIONAL GEOGRAPHIC MAGAZINE

MELVILLE BELL GROSVENOR Editor-in-Chief and Board Chairman
MELVIN M. PAYNE President of the Society

GILBERT M. GROSVENOR Editor

FRANC SHOR, JOHN SCOFIELD Associate Editors

Senior Assistant Editors
James Cerruti, W. E. Garrett, Kenneth MacLeish
Jules B. Billard, Allan C. Fisher, Jr.

Assistant Editors: Andrew H. Brown, Joseph Judge, Edward J. Linehan, Samuel W. Matthews, Carolyn Bennett Patterson, Howell Walker, Kenneth F. Weaver
Senior Editorial Staff: William S. Ellis, Rowe Findley, William Graves, Bryan Hodgson, Robert P. Jordan, Nathaniel T. Kenney, Bart McDowell, John J. Putman, Gordon Young; Senior Scientist: Paul A. Zahl
Foreign Editorial Staff: Luis Marden (Chief); Thomas J. Abercrombie, David S. Boyer, Howard La Fay, Volkmar Wentzel, Peter T. White
Editorial Staff: Harvey Arden, Kent Britt, Thomas Y. Canby, Louis de la Haba, Mike W. Edwards, Noel Grove, Alice J. Hall, Werner Janney, Jerry Kline, Michael E. Long, John L. McIntosh, Elizabeth A. Moize, Ethel A. Starbird
Editorial Layout: Howard E. Paine (Chief); Charles C. Uhl
Geographic Art: William N. Palmstrom (Chief). *Artists:* Lisa Biganzoli, William H. Bond, John W. Lothers, Robert C. Magis, Ned M. Seidler. *Cartographic Artists:* Victor J. Kelley, Snejinka Stefanoff. *Research:* Walter Q. Crowe (Supervisor), Virginia L. Baza, George W. Beatty, John D. Garst, Dorothy A. Nicholson, Isaac Ortiz (Production)
Research: Margaret G. Bledsoe (Chief); Ann K. Wendt (Associate Chief); Newton V. Blakeslee (Assistant Chief for Geographic Information), Carolyn H. Anderson, Susan L. Anderson, Bette Joan Goss, Jan Holderness, Lesley B. Lane, Levenia Loder, Jean B. McConville, Carol M. McNamara, Susan F. Moore, Frances H. Parker. *Correspondence:* Carolyn F. Clewell, Clifford R. DuBois
Library: Virginia Carter Hills (Librarian); Patricia Murphy Smith (Assistant Librarian), Louise A. Robinson
Editorial Administration: Joyce W. McKean, Assistant to the Editor; Virginia H. Finnegan, Winifred M. Myers, Shirley Neff, M. Jean Vile (Editorial Assistants); Dorothy M. Corson (Indexes); Evelyn Fox, Dolores Kennedy (Travel); Jeanne S. Duiker, Lorie Wendling, Mary Anne McMillen (Records)
ILLUSTRATIONS STAFF: *Illustrations Editor:* Herbert S. Wilburn, Jr. *Associate Illustrations Editor:* Thomas R. Smith. *Art Editor:* Andrew Poggenpohl. *Assistant Illustrations Editors:* David L. Arnold, O. Louis Mazzatenta, Charlene Murphy, Robert S. Patton, Elie S. Rogers, W. Allan Royce, Jon Schneeberger, Mary Griswold Smith. *Layout and Production:* H. Edward Kim (Chief). *Picture Editor:* Bruce A. McElfresh. *Research:* Paula C. Simmons, Barbara A. Shattuck (Asst.). *Librarian:* L. Fern Dame, *Assistant Librarian:* Carolyn J. Harrison
Engraving and Printing: Dee J. Andella (Chief); John R. Metcalfe, William W. Smith, James R. Whitney
PHOTOGRAPHIC STAFF: *Director of Photography:* Robert E. Gilka. *Assistant Directors:* Dean Conger, Joseph J. Scherschel. *Photographers:* James L. Amos, James P. Blair, Victor R. Boswell, Jr., Bruce Dale, Dick Durrance II, Gordon W. Gahan, Otis Imboden, Emory Kristof, Bates Littlehales, Robert W. Madden, George F. Mobley, Robert S. Oakes, Winfield Parks, Robert F. Sisson (Natural Science), James L. Stanfield. Lilian Davidson (Administration). *Film Review:* Guy W. Starling (Chief). *Photographic Equipment:* John E. Fletcher (Chief), Donald McBain.
Photographic Services: Carl M. Shrader (Chief); Milton A. Ford (Associate Chief); Jon R. Adams, Herbert Altemus, Jr., David H. Chisman, Lawrence F. Ludwig (Assistant Chief, Phototypography), Claude E. Petrone, J. Fran Pyles, Jr., Donald E. Stemper; Joan S. Simms (Asst.)

RELATED EDUCATIONAL SERVICES OF THE SOCIETY

Cartography: William T. Peele (Chief); David W. Cook (Associate Chief) *Cartographic Staff:* Margery K. Barkdull, Charles F. Case, Ted Dachter Richard J. Darley, John F. Dorr, Russel G. Fritz, Richard R. Furno, Charles W. Gotthardt, Jr., Catherine M. Hart, Donald A. Jaeger, Harry D. Kauhan James W. Killion, Manuela G. Kogutowicz, Charles L. Miller, David Moore, Robert W. Northrop, Richard K. Rogers, John F. Shupe, Charles Stern, Douglas A. Strobel, George E. Stuart (Archeology), Tibor G. Tot Thomas A. Wall, Thomas A. Walsh
Books: Merle Severy (Chief); Seymour L. Fishbein (Assistant Chief), Thomas B. Allen, Ross Bennett, Charles O. Hyman, Anne Dirkes Kobor, David Robinson, Wilhelm R. Saake, Verla Lee Smith
Special Publications and Educational Filmstrips: Robert L. Breeden (Chief) Donald J. Crump (Asst. Chief), William L. Allen, Josephine B. Bolt, David R. Bridge, Linda Bridge, Margery G. Dunn, Johanna G. Farren, Ronald Fisher, William R. Gray, Mary Ann Harrell, Margaret McKelway Johnson Geraldine Linder, Robert Messer, H. Robert Morrison, Cynthia Ramsay Ann Crouch Resh, Philip B. Silcott, Tee Loftin Snell, Joseph A. Taney George V. White, Merrill Windsor
Recording Division: John M. Lavery (Chief)
School Service: Ralph Gray (Chief and Editor of National Geographic School Bulletin); Charles H. Sloan (Assistant Chief). Joseph B. Goodwin, Ellen Jo Hurst, Veronica Smith, Janis Knudsen Wheat
News Service: Windsor P. Booth (Chief); Paul Sampson (Assistant Chief) Donald J. Frederick, William J. O'Neill, Robert C. Radcliffe; Isabel Clark
Television and Educational Films: Dennis B. Kane (Chief); Sidney Platt (Supervisor, Educational Projects); David Cooper, Carl W. Harmon, Jr., Arthur Miller, Jr., Patricia F. Northrop; Marjorie M. Moomey (Chief of Research)
Lectures: Joanne M. Hess (Chief); Robert G. Fleegal, Mary W. McKinney Gerald L. Wiley, Carl E. Ziebe
Explorers Hall: T. Keilor Bentley (Curator-Director)
EUROPEAN OFFICE: W. Edward Roscher (Associate Secretary and Director) Jennifer Moseley (Assistant), 4 Curzon Place, Mayfair, London, W1Y 8EJ
ADVERTISING: *Director:* William A. Boeger, Jr. *Assistant Director:* James Till. *National Advertising Manager:* William Turgeon, 1251 Ave. of Americas, New York, N.Y. 10020. *Regional managers—Eastern:* George W. Kellner, New York. *Midwestern:* Robert R. Henn, Chicago. *West Thomas Martz, San Francisco. Los Angeles:* Jack Wallace. *Canada:* Robert W. Horan, New York. *Automotive:* John F. Grant, New York. *Travel:* George A. Van Splinter, New York. *European Director:* Richard V. Macy, 21 Jean-Mermoz, Paris 8e, France. *Production:* E. M. Pusey, Jr.